Lancelot Andrewes
and his
Private Devotions

Alexander Whyte
translator

BAKER BOOK HOUSE
Grand Rapids, Michigan 49506

Reprinted 1981 by Baker Book House Company
from the Second Edition (1895) published by
Oliphant, Anderson, and Ferrier

ISBN: 0-8010-0176-5

FOREWORD

The fact that one of the great devotional classics has, in the recent past, been largely unavailable has been an occasion for sorrow. *Lancelot Andrewes and His Private Devotions* has meant so much to me that I have desired to share this written word with as many as possible. That Bishop Andrewes was a spiritual giant, there is no doubt, and that his deepest insights were put into writing is a blessing of the highest order. Ever since, years ago, I was introduced to Andrewes by the words of T. S. Eliot, this classic volume has been a treasured part of my own library. Now, because of the imaginative effort of Dr. Ralph Turnbull and Baker Book House, I can share the treasure far and wide. For this I am grateful.

Bishop Andrewes loved the church, but he also recognized the dangers inherent in any ecclesiastical structure. Accordingly, more than once he prayed for both the continuance and the reformation of the church. In an unforgettable conjunction of phrases he prayed God to "supply what is wanting" and to "strengthen what remains." This is a prayer in which we can still join after more than 350 years. A true classic is never out of date.

The theological insights represented in Andrewes' private prayers are priceless. A good example of such profundity concerns man's responsibility for sin. The abiding paradox of sin is that *we* are to blame for it, but we cannot, of ourselves, heal it! God did not cause

FOREWORD

it, but He can forgive and overcome it. Heresy comes from the denial of either side of the paradox.

> Take away from me that which I have made.
> Let that which Thou hast made remain in me.

No sensitive reader can fail to be touched by Andrewes' sense of sharing in the needs of all sorts and conditions of men. He prayed for kings, but he also prayed for "prisoners," "foreigners," those "troubled by unclean spirits," and many more. He has helped me so much in this regard that I wish to share his enlargement of Christian charity with as many new readers as the present publication can reach.

D. ELTON TRUEBLOOD

THE Transcript of Andrewes's *Private Devotions* contained in this volume was made with the current Greek and Latin printed texts and with the translations of Drake, Stanhope, Hall, Newman, Neale, and Venables, as well as that of a private hand, before the transcriber. Newman's translation from the Greek is above praise, and it is enough to say of Neale's translation from the Latin that it is not unworthy to stand beside Newman's English. It will be seen that free use has been made of both; but it seemed peculiarly fitting, in a work so largely scriptural in its phraseology, that preference should be given, wherever possible, to the matchless language of the Authorised Version, in the production of which Bishop Andrewes had so large a share. Certain other modifications in the Transcript have their authority in the lately recovered and exceedingly valuable Laudian text, edited by Canon Medd and published by the Society for the Promotion of Christian Knowledge, which still waits for translation. The Biography and the Interpretation were delivered as opening lectures to classes formed this session for the study of some of the great mystical, spiritual, and devotional writers.

St. George's Free Church,
    Edinburgh, *November* 1895.

The transcriber and his friends who worked with him did their best for the First Edition ; but the Second Edition is in many parts considerably improved.

December 1895.

CONTENTS

Meditations and Prayers for various times
    and seasons :—

Communion Prayers and Meditations :—

A BIOGRAPHY

LANCELOT ANDREWES was born the son of a sea- Andrewes.
faring man at Allhallows Barking, London, in
1555, and he died Bishop of Winchester at South-
wark in 1626. Andrewes was born one year
after Hooker, four years before Isaac Casaubon His
and Robert Bruce, six years before Bacon, nine Contem-
poraries.
years before Shakespeare, eleven years before
James the First, and eighteen years before Laud
and Donne. Lancelot Andrewes lives to us
and shines to us to this day in his *Private
Devotions.* All our interest in Andrewes is centred The *Devo-
tions.*
in his *Private Devotions.* Andrewes was a great
scholar and a great patron of poor scholars, he
was the most popular preacher of his day, in
his hospitality he was the pattern of an apostolic
bishop, and he was a great favourite with his
king; but all that would have been forgotten
by us long ago had it not been for his one incomparable and immortal book, the *Private Devotions.*
We carry Andrewes's *Private Devotions* in our
mind as we read of his birth, of his education, of
his talents, of his industry, of his rise in life, and
of all his after-career. Our interest in Andrewes's
scholarship and wide reading, in his churchman-
ship and in his statesmanship, in his single life,
in his friends and in his opponents, in his great
opportunities and in his great temptations, both
as a minister of Jesus Christ and as a privy
councillor of King James,—our interest in all that
is awakened and is intensely quickened as we

study, and much more as we ourselves employ, his *Private Devotions*. With that entrancing book open before us we search the histories and the biographies of his time; the home and the foreign politics of his time; the State papers, the Church controversies, and not least the Court scandals and the criminal reports of his time, with the keenest interest and the most solicitous anxiety. 'I am wonderful curious,' says Montaigne, 'to discover and know the mind, the soul, the genuine disposition, and the natural judgment of my authors; but much more what they do in their chambers and in their closets than what they are in the senate and in the market-place.' And that is just what we discover and know of our author in his *Private Devotions*. We have preserved to us in that priceless book what Andrewes was in his chamber and in his closet as we have no other author preserved to us in any other book that I know. To Andrewes more than to any other man that I know has this assurance of our Saviour been to the letter fulfilled,—But thou, when thou prayest, enter into thy closet, and when thou hast shut thy door, pray to thy Father which is in secret; and thy Father which seeth in secret shall reward thee openly. For, what Andrewes prayed for in his closet, and how he prayed for it, all the world now openly knows and openly has the reward of.

At School and College.

As soon as young Andrewes had a book put into his hands he began to show a quite extraordinary aptitude for the acquisition of languages. All his days Andrewes never could write the English language with any beauty or purity or good taste, but there seems to have been no language under

heaven that he could not read. Andrewes proved
himself a perfect genius and paragon as often as he
had another grammar and another dictionary put
into his hands, but when he took up a pen to
compose in his own language all his talent would
seem to have forsaken him and fled. There is
scholarship, and there is the sense of beauty and
the taste for letters that should surely come from
all sound scholarship, and some men have the
excellent taste without the scholarship, while other
men have all the scholarship with nothing whatever
of the fine taste or the sweet sensibility for good
writing. Shakespeare in that day had little Latin
and less Greek, but what English Shakespeare
wrote! While Andrewes had all the Latin and
all the Greek and everything else that his great
contemporary had so little of, and yet what poor
work he made in the noble tongue of Cranmer and
North and Shakespeare and Hooker and Bacon.
But what we have to do with at his present stage
is Andrewes's wonderful facility in mastering the
ancient languages as well as the foreign languages
of his own day. From his tender years, Isaacson,
his secretary and biographer, tells us, Andrewes
was totally addicted to the study of languages; and
in his youth there appeared in him such aptness to
learn, answerable to his endeavours, that his first
two schoolmasters contended who should have the
honour of his breeding. By his extraordinary
industry and admirable capacity he soon outstripped
all his school-fellows, having become an excellent
Grecian and Hebrician. When he came home to
London from Cambridge for the Easter holiday, he
was wont to bespeak a tutor for those vacant weeks
till he went back to his college after a month's

absence a much better scholar than he had been
when he left it. Isaacson had often heard the
reverend and worthy prelate say that when he was
a young scholar at the University, and so all his
time onwards, he never loved or used any games or
ordinary recreation, either within doors, as cards,
dice, tables, chess, or the like : or abroad, as butts,
quoits, bowls, or any such ; but his ordinary exercise
and recreation was walking either alone by himself,
or with some selected companion, with whom he
might confer, argue, and recount their studies.   He
would often profess that to observe the grass, herbs,
corn, trees, cattle, earth, waters, heavens, any of
the creatures, and to contemplate their natures,
orders, qualities, virtues, uses, and such like, was
ever to him the greatest mirth, content, and recreation that could be : and this he held to his
dying day.   'He accounted all that time lost that
he spent not in his studie,' says Bishop Buckeridge,
'wherein in learning he outstript all his equals,
and his indefatigable industry had almost outstript
himself : he studied so hard when others played,
that if his parents and masters had not forced him
to play with them also, all the play had been
marred.'   And then Fuller follows Isaacson and
Buckeridge with this,—that 'the world wanted learning to know how learned this man was ; so skilled
in all (especially Oriental) languages, that some con-
ceive he might, if then living, almost have served as
an interpreter-general at the confusion of tongues.'
' His admirable knowledge in the learned tongues,
adds Buckeridge, ' Latine, Greek, Hebrew, Chaldee,
Syriack, Arabick, besides other modern tongues to
the number of fifteen, as I am informed, was such,
and so rare, that he may well be ranked to be in

the first place, to be one of the rarest linguists in Christendom.'

No young man of that day ran a more brilliant In Holy Orders. career than that career was which Andrewes ran, and his Christian character kept full pace with all his attainments and all his promotions. Scholar and Fellow of Pembroke, Vicar of St Giles', Cripplegate, Prebendary, first of Southwell and then of St Paul's, Master of his College, Chaplain to Whitgift and to Queen Elizabeth, and Dean of Westminster: through all these upward steps Andrewes rapidly rose, leaving behind him on each successive stage a record of most excellent work accomplished, and carrying with him a most honourable and a much-beloved name. 'The course of his studies,' says Sir John Harrington, 'was not, as most men's are in these times, to get a little superficial divinity by reading two or three of the new writers, and straight take orders and up into the pulpit. Dr Andrewes gathered before he spent, reading both new writers and old writers, and not as tasting them, but as digesting them.' Out of that great storehouse of that time, Hacket's *Life of Archbishop Williams*, we gather abundant proof that as Dean of Westminster and superintendent of its famous school Andrewes was still the same scholar, and the same lover of scholarship, he had been when he was at school himself. Hacket, happily, was himself at Westminster at that time, and this is the fine tribute that he pays to the learned dean's great industry and great care over his young scholars: 'How strict that excellent man was to charge our masters,' says Hacket, 'that they should give us lessons out of none but the most classical authors; he did often supply the place both of head schoolmaster and usher for the space of a whole week together, and gave us not an hour of loitering time from morning to night : he caused our exercises in prose and verse to be brought to him, to examine our style and proficiency; he never walked to Chiswick for his recreation without a brace of this young fry ; and in that wayfaring leisure had a singular dexterity to fill those narrow vessels with a funnel. And sometimes thrice a week, sometimes oftener, he sent for the uppermost scholars to his lodging at night, and kept them with him from eight till eleven, unfolding to them the best rudiments of the Greek tongue, and the elements of the Hebrew Grammar; and all this he did to us boys without any compulsion of correction, nay, I never heard him utter so much as a word of austerity among us. This great and good prelate,' Hacket gratefully adds, 'was the first that planted me in my tender studies, and watered them continually with his great bounty.'

The Dean of Westminster had a leading hand in the production of the Authorised Version of the English Bible, 'a work,' says Dr Perry, 'which has gone far to redeem King James from the contempt and reprobation of posterity.' A new translation of the Bible had been moved for by Reynolds at the famous Hampton Court Conference in 1604, and though on all the other matters discussed at the Conference the king went against Reynolds and the Puritan side, yet in this matter, and in spite of Bancroft's opposition, James accepted Reynolds's proposal. The king, no doubt, had the assistance of some of the leading divines of that day in making the excellent arrangements for the work

The
English
Bible.

of the translation, and in drawing up the admirable instructions to the translators that were issued in his name; but to take the side he did take when the proposal was made, and to put his royal name to the arrangements made and to the instructions sent out,—all that greatly redounds to the king's credit. Andrewes was one of the secretaries of the Translation Company, and it is more than probable that the rules and instructions that were issued to the translators came from his scholarly pen. Certain it is that an immense amount of correspondence, and of many other kinds of work, fell to the dean's hands during the four years over which this great task extended. 'But that this afternoon is our translation time, and that most of our company are negligent, I would have come to you,' he writes to the secretary of the Society of Antiquaries, of which society he had at that time just been made a member. The whole Translation Company consisted of forty-seven of the leading scholars and divines of England, both prelatic and puritan. They sat in six committees, and the books of the Old and New Testaments were divided out among them. The first committee, which sat at Westminster, had the Sacred Books from Genesis to the end of Second Kings allotted to them, and the dean's name stands at the head of the Westminster committee. 'And now,' says Fuller, writing of the year 1611, 'after long expectation and great desire, came forth the new translation of the Bible, most beautifully printed, by a select and competent number of divines, to whom by their industry, skilfulness, piety, and discretion the Church is bound in a debt of special remembrance and thankfulness. These, with a Jacob, rolled away the stone from the mouth of the well of life, so that now even Rachels, weak women, may freely come, both to drink themselves and to water the flocks of their families at the same. Leave we these worthy men, of whom, as also of that gracious king that employed them, we may say, Wheresoever the Bible shall be preached or read in the whole world, there shall also this that they have done be told in memorial of them.'

Bishop of Chichester.

With his elevation to the bench of bishops that sad drop and deterioration of Andrewes's character began which cannot be kept hid from any unprejudiced reader of his life, and which stands written out in a sea of tears the bitterness of which every reader of sensibility must surely taste on every page of his penitential *Devotions*. A more servile and short-sighted body of men than the bench of bishops under James the First never set a royal house on the road to ruin; and with all his saintliness, and with all his unworldliness, Lancelot Andrewes at last consented to sit down among them. 'He contrived to live at Court while contemning the world.' George Herbert writes of the same court: 'I now look back upon my aspiring thoughts, and think myself more happy than if I had attained what then I so ambitiously thirsted for. And I now can behold the court with an impartial eye, and see plainly that it is made up of fraud, and titles, and flattery, and many other such empty, imaginary, painted pleasures.' 'A main cause of all the misery and mischief in our land is the fearfullest of flattery of our prelates and clergy,' says one of the Rev. Joseph Mead's correspondents in 1623. It is only those who truly love Andrewes,—and as Buckeridge who had known him for thirty years says, 'I loved him, but yet my love doth not blind or outsway my judgment,'—it is only those, I say, who have long known and who truly love Andrewes, and who have his *Devotions* day and night in their hands till they come to owe him their own souls, it is only they who will feel the full pain and shame of Lancelot Andrewes's position as a minister of Jesus Christ, and at the same time a Privy-Councillor and a Court favourite of James the First. The truth is, no man could remain a man at all, and much less a man of Christian honour and uncompromised integrity, at the Court and in the favour of James. What a system of things that was which placed the Church of Christ and her chief ministers, as well as the whole people of a great and growing nation, under the heel of a man like James Stuart! The strongest men bent and broke under the dreadful incubus of that abominable system. It was only one outstanding man here and another outstanding man there who could remain true and upright and honourable men under that abominable system. It was only a statesman like Bristol, and a judge like Coke, and a bishop like Abbot, and a minister like Robert Bruce who could live through such an atmosphere. The best and the most blameless men became compromised, corrupted, and demoralised. And that a man of Andrewes's goodness and beauty of character was so compromised, corrupted, and demoralised is surely of itself sufficient condemnation of James and of the life of his Court, and of that whole abominable system of things that had grafted the sword and the sceptre of England upon the crook of Jesus Christ, and then had put all three into the hand of James the First. The

time had been when you would have seen Lancelot
Andrewes rather have his right hand cut off than
that it should countersign any king's command in
such an infamous affair as the divorce case of the
Earl and Countess of Essex. But ten years at a
Stuart Court had brought even Lancelot Andrewes
down to that. If you cannot so much as touch
pitch without being defiled, how could you expect
to wade about in a pit of pitch for half a lifetime
and come out clean? The Essex case is much too
loathsome to be more than merely mentioned here,
and I do not wonder that Mr Gardiner protests
that nothing short of direct evidence will suffice to
convince him that Lancelot Andrewes knew what
he was doing when he took the side he did take
in the Essex case. Mr Gardiner has had all the
evidence before him, and he is both an able and a
just judge; but, much as I would like to see
Andrewes cleared, or even given the benefit of a
doubt in the Essex case, I despair of ever having
the relief of mind of seeing that done. I have read
far too much direct evidence against Andrewes for
my own full faith and perfect pride in Andrewes.
The successive state trials connected with that long-
lasting, wide-spreading, and utterly loathsome case,
supplemented and aggravated as they are by the
powerful Memorial and outspoken Speech of Archbishop Abbot, to all of which I shall always be compelled to add some of the most agonising pages of the
Private Devotions—all that is nothing short of over-
whelming evidence to me. Had Bishop Andrewes
kept a private diary, and had he kept his diary as his
disciple and friend Archbishop Laud kept his; that
is to say, had Andrewes entered his 'unfortunate-
nesses' and his 'ill-haps' under fast days and in

The Essex
Case.

cyphers and in initials as the Archbishop did, I
cannot doubt what some of those cyphers and
initials would have been, nor how 'slubbered' they
would have been 'with his pious hands, and watered
with his penitential tears.' 'Some great calamity
happens to you, you do very well to make it an
occasion of exercising a great devotion,' says William
Law.

Much as I should like to agree with Mr Gardiner
in the hesitation and judicial doubt of which he gives
Andrewes's memory the benefit, I am compelled
in this matter to side rather with Mark Pattison
and with many other students of that time as to
the depth of the infamy into which Bishop Andrewes
slipped and fell when James summoned him to vote,
and pursued after him and compelled him to vote
on the King's side, which was also the wanton's
side, of the Essex case. I would not have come
near that noisome ditch unless I had seen Bishop
Andrewes's footsteps being dragged up toward it in
a leash of servility till he all but sank out of sight
under it. Shall I, to please King James and to
shelter and satisfy his vile favourites,—shall I send
my soul to hell! shouted Archbishop Abbot to one
of the king's emissaries. No! I will not do it. But
Bishop Andrewes did it. And Bishop Andrewes's
soul is still in hell to the end of his life, and a
hundred times in his remorseful *Devotions,* because
he did it. There is no other word for it. For a
man like Lancelot Andrewes to have to look back
all his days, and that too from an episcopal throne,
to that scandalous Essex case, and to see himself
in the society, if not in the secrets, of James, and
Rochester, and the Countess of Essex, and Mrs
Turner, and Bishop Neill,—out of the belly of hell

cried I! As whoredom and wine take away the heart, so do servility and party spirit, the fear of kings and the respect of great men. But as David's heart came back to him from adultery and murder in the Fifty-first Psalm, so did Bishop Andrewes's heart come back to him from servility and sycophancy and the sale of justice in many a confession and in many a commendation of his *Private Devotions*. If I did not believe absolutely in the sincerity and the truthfulness of Andrewes's repentance in every literal syllable and down to the blackest bottom of his *Private Devotions*, I would not have opened my mouth or taken up my pen about him. But, absolutely and utterly believing that Andrewes means all that he says when he is on his knees clothed in sackcloth and with dust on his head and a rope round his neck, I am not afraid at the worst thing that I meet with in his previous life. 'Come,' says Andrewes, 'and hear, all ye that fear God, and I will declare what He hath done for my soul. Blessed be God, which hath not turned away my prayer, nor His mercy from me.'

Visit to Scotland.

Continuing thus fearlessly to trace all Bishop Andrewes's footprints to the end of his life, I was led to open the eleventh volume of Professor Masson's Privy Council Register of Scotland, which is full of His Most Sacred Majesty's long-promised visit to his native land. And what has burned itself most bitterly into my memory and my heart out of that visit was not his royal determination that Scotland should there and then set aside her accustomed and conscientious forms of public worship and of Church government at his kingly word; what made my blood boil as I read it was the way that the gentry and the farmers and the poor labourers were requisitioned and robbed right and left by the

royal progress through this country. James had
now been for fourteen years the absolute owner of
a land so rich that the poverty of Scotland was a
proverb and a jest at his dissolute and ribald Court;
but, with all that, James at that moment was up to
the lips in public and in personal debt : and that
not by building cathedrals and fitting out fleets, but
by fattening his favourites and making rich and
licentious men of all who fawned on him and
flattered him. Those were the days of the loyal
benevolences. 'A benevolence,' says Dr Murray,
'was a forced loan levied without legal authority.
First so called in 1473 when astutely asked for by
Edward iv. as a token of goodwill towards his rule.'
'A benevolence,' said Lord Digby, in the Long
Parliament, 'which is a malevolence indeed.' But
before we blame James and his impoverished
ministers too much for their benevolences in
England and for their requisitions in Scotland, let
us hear all that they had been doing of late in order
to raise money. 'Everything,' says Dr Perry, 'was
sold that could be sold, everything that could attract a buyer. Patents, monopolies, offices, dignities
were all in the market. Knighthood had become
such a drug that it could be had for sixty pounds.
Even church dignities were to be had at a cheap
price.' And now to return to Scotland. You cannot
imagine the misery that the king's visit caused the
poor country on which James descended, not indeed
with the six thousand of a train he had so royally
requisitioned for, but still with sufficient to drive
the poor people mad who had to transport and feed
the king and his enormous retinue wherever he
signified his royal will to go, and as long as he
honoured them with his stay. From Berwick to

Edinburgh, from Edinburgh to Perth, from Perth to St Andrews, from St Andrews to Stirling, and from Stirling to Glasgow; every name calls up the most tyrannical acts on the part of the king and his ecclesiastical abettors. But what has burned itself still more into my indignation was the Privy Council demands on the people, the same Privy Council of which James did Andrewes the honour to make him a member. As I read the council papers with my eye upon the object, I found myself calling out, What, in the name of his Divine Master, was Bishop Andrewes doing away from his proper work, and travelling about in the train of this royal freebooter? He has some pungent passages in his *Devotions* about defrauding the poor of their wages. Were those passages set down as he remembered in remorse how he and his king had been carried about and feasted and amused from place to place in Scotland, where Laud complained that he found no religion, but where the poor heathen had to find James and Andrewes and Laud and all the rest in horses and carriages and in royal board and lodging on pain of the halter?

His Sermons.

Andrewes preached one of his least pedantic sermons, and one with less than usual of his 'ingenious idleness' in it, before James in Holyrood Chapel during that royal visit to our city. The Edinburgh people even in that day were severe judges of sermons, and the king's favourite preacher did not escape the searching climate he had come to. 'How did you like the sermon this morning?' James was still Scotsman enough to ask of a Presbyterian lord who had been present at the service. 'No doubt your Majesty's bishop is a learned man, but he cannot preach. He rather plays with his text than preaches on it.' And I must say that I entirely agree with my outspoken fellow-countryman against all the adulation that has been lavished on Andrewes's preaching from that day to this. Canon Mozley, who came to be one of the clearest-headed and profoundest writers of our generation, has a preposterously extravagant paper on Andrewes's Sermons, in the *British Critic* for January 1842. The whole paper is a set and a highly elaborated eulogy in which such overworked words are applied to Andrewes's sermons as these :— force, animation, depth, fertility, felicity, admirable decision and completeness, quickness, variety, dexterity, richness, rapidity, ubiquity, clear-headed-ness, manifoldness, what he is going to say occupies him, what he is saying he only says and no more,—language which, were it distributed upon Hooker's sermons and Taylor's and Newman's and Robertson's, would yield a sufficiency of epithet for all the four. After Mozley has written himself out of breath, he settles down to say that 'these characteristics of Bishop Andrewes are not plainly discernible, we allow, at first sight.' No, they are not. Nor, I am sincerely sorry to say, have they been discerned at all by one who has looked for them longer and oftener than he would like to confess. My sight and experience of Andrewes's sermons was at first and still is rather that of one who is said to have set a high value upon some others of Andrewes's writings, but who, at the same time, had the detachment from party spirit and the intellectual integrity to say,—'I own that however clear-headed I might be when I sat down to read one of his sermons, I invariably rose at the conclusion of it with my brain bewildered and confused.' But the *British Critic* and its young Anglo-Catholics were all engaged in that day in writing up, without rhyme or reason, the churchmen of James's and Charles's day; and with much of a high, a fine, and a quite singular distinction, at the same time less theological openness, less true catholicity, and less fair and just judgment you will scarcely meet with anywhere than just in their sectarian and reactionary writings. Archdeacon Hare is the only writer of any authority and eminence I know on whom the good sense and sound judgment of that ancient Scottish lord has descended. I have read a good many sermons in my time, and there are some sufficiently High Church sermons that I have continually in my hands. It cannot then be their church doctrine, or their church tone, or their exclusive temper that has turned me so often away from Andrewes's sermons. And still as I read again about Andrewes, and as his editors and biographers and fellow-churchmen praise his sermons, I go back to his five volumes, accusing myself that I cannot have done them and myself proper justice,—but always with the same result. I tried to read the Gowrie series again one Sabbath morning above the fiord of Mandal in Norway during my late holiday time till I could read no longer, I so felt as I read that I was wasting and desecrating the Lord's Day. I threw down the eight maledictory sermons preached before James on the long dead and buried Gowrie brothers, and took up to give it another trial the much-praised sermon on Justification; and to do it justice I took paper and pencil determined to bring something home to you out of it. But with the old result. The doctrine was all right, when I got at it. The doctrine was the Pauline, Lutheran, Puritan, Presbyterian, only possible doctrine on that text and on that topic, but the magnificent doctrine never kindled the preacher, never gave him wings, never carried him away, never fused nor took the slag out of his style, never made him once eloquent, never to the end of his sermon made him a great preacher of a great gospel. I felt sorry I had not brought with me the third volume of Keble's Hooker, such was my hunger for Hooker's greatest sermon after those twenty tantalising pages of his unimproved contemporary. But, happily, I had brought Mr Henry Craik's *English Prose Selections* with me, the first volume of which contains ten pieces out of Hooker with Mr Vernon Blackburn's perfect little paper prefixed. Ay, that is preaching, I exclaimed to myself as I read and read again the four golden pages taken out of Hooker's golden sermon. That is writing. That is English. That is the best of gospels in the best of English. Yes, when I go back to Edinburgh, and have my classes again before me, I shall command them to master Hooker, at any rate on Justification, such is his style in that immortal sermon, his depth, his strength, and his sublimity. I shall also set Andrewes's *Devotions* day and night before them,—but not his sermons. Bruce's and Hooker's and Donne's and Taylor's and Leighton's, and many other sermons since their day, but not Andrewes's. Whoever says otherwise, the blunt, uncourtly Scottish lord was right. We are assured on all hands that the bishop's delivery was 'inimitable.' But substance and unction have always come before delivery in Scotland. Andrewes is a learned man, and, better than that, he can pray as no other man can pray, but he cannot preach, to be called preaching. That dissatisfied Edinburgh lord most likely was one of Robert Bruce's elders, and he must have heard that 'stately Presbyterian divine' preach his famous Five Sermons on the Lord's Supper, and his Six Sermons on King Hezekiah's Sickness, and his taste for a sermon must have been formed on the model of that preacher of such distinction. And if I had the ear of one of Bishop Andrewes's descendants in church doctrine and in English preaching I should earnestly advise him to send to Edinburgh for Robert Bruce's Sermons. He would find in that noble volume what we in Scotland believe to be the true New Testament teaching on the Lord's Supper, and he would see that doctrine put forward in an ancient Scottish style not wholly unworthy of the great subject. Keble gives us at the end of his Hooker a sermon of Hooker's which was found among Bishop Andrewes's papers. Found in such company, it was as if a sermon of Newman's had got in among Simeon's skeletons. It is enough for one man that he can pray as Andrewes alone can pray, but let no beginner in the pulpit go to Andrewes to learn how to preach.

It is no blame to Andrewes that he cannot preach like Bruce or Hooker or Donne or Taylor; great preachers like them are born and not made. But no man has any business to tune and tamper with his pulpit to please either his king or his congregation, and a true preacher will never do it. I do not complain of Andrewes because I find his sermons unreadable and unprofitable, but I cannot excuse him for his Gowrie and Gunpowder Plot series, and too many other sermons like them. Could James not have got some other of his Court

Chaplains to curse the hanged and dismembered Gowries every fifth of August, and leave Andrewes to his proper work and to his private prayers? But no. James, born fool as he was in some things, was a shrewd enough sovereign in some other things, and he knew quite well what he was doing when he commanded Lancelot Andrewes in England, while never all he could do could command Robert Bruce in Scotland, to preach or to pray to his policy and to his passions. What a pity it is, I have sometimes exclaimed to myself, that anything of Andrewes's has been preserved besides his *Devotions*! And yet, may it not have been so ordained in order to comfort and assure us every night when we have to go with a continual confession that is such a continual condemnation and such a continual contrast to our everyday life. 'O God,' prayed Andrewes in secret every night, 'save me from making a god of the king.' On this whole matter the simple truth is that the plainest facts of history and of biography in Andrewes's case have been so twisted about and so covered up by party spirit and ecclesiastical pride that it is impossible to draw them out into any light of day without great pain and great regret. But what has here been said has this for it at any rate, that it was a very unwelcome and a very distressing discovery to the present speaker when he made it. It seemed to him like laying hands on one's own father, as some one has said it somewhere in Plato.

Lancelot Andrewes was a fast-rising scholar of Bacon. Pembroke when Francis Bacon went up to Trinity in the 'pregnancy and towardness of his wit,' a boy between twelve and thirteen years of age. And Lord Bacon's name comes afterwards to be the symbol of so much, that we like to think of two such men as Andrewes and Bacon being early and lifelong friends. And, though I do not know that we have documents for it, I like to think of the elder scholar selecting the younger and taking him out to those country walks and talks that Isaacson has told us so delightfully about. That the rising divine and the pushing young lawyer were intimate friends early in life we have abundant evidence. Mr Spedding, who has unearthed everything that exists about Bacon, has produced an invitation that Bacon sent to Andrewes when he was preacher in St Giles', Cripplegate, asking him to come out to Twickenham to share a holiday with a party of young lawyers and other scholars. But Andrewes's pulpit duties detained him at home. Andrewes all his days loved good society and a hospitable table, but not till his day's work was done. Throughout life, Bacon's biographer assures us, the Lord Chancellor held the bishop in special reverence. Indeed, there is nothing either in Andrewes's best life or in his best work that gives us such a high idea of his intellect as the fact that Bacon submitted *The Advancement of Learning* and some others of his magnificent books to Andrewes, calling him his inquisitor, and asking him for his criticisms and corrections. 'You were wont to make me believe that you took a liking to my writings; will you therefore mark what you think not current in my style, or harsh to credit and opinion, or inconvenient to the position of the writer. For to write at one's ease,' as Bacon said to Casaubon about another book of his, 'that which others are to read at their ease is of little consequence. The contemplations I have in view are those which may bring about the better ordering of man's life and business with all its turmoil. How great an enterprise is this, and with what small help I have attempted it.' This of Bacon leads us into his Private Memoranda, where we see him laying his lines to ' fish for testaments,' for loans, for gifts, for bribes, and indeed for anything and everything that would bring in money to a poor man who had taken all knowledge for his province, a province, as he often sadly said, that would take a king or a pope to occupy and hold it. Bacon sets it down among other like secret plots against his best friends,—'not desisting to draw in Bishop Andrewes, he being single, rych, and sickly.' 'Bacon's was a mind,' says Dr Abbott, 'unique and extraordinary; worldly, it is true, but not after the common fashion of worldliness; say rather an unworldly mind of superhuman magnanimity, gradually becoming enslaved by the world while professing to use the world as a mere tool. Bacon will place all the arts of worldliness at the feet of Truth, and will master them by first obeying them.' 'A man whose fall,' as the same writer so truly and so finely says, ' shook men's confidence in humanity.'

Broken in health and broken in heart as Bacon might well be by a fall that shook the world, and the terrible shock of which we still feel to this day, Bacon died at his desk. And, though Andrewes had sat on his trial and had acquiesced in his sentence, Bacon continues to acquaint Andrewes with all his intended work, and consults him about it to the end. Bacon's *Holy War* is not Bunyan's book of the same name. 'There cannot but ensue a dissolution of the state of the Turk, whereof the time seemeth to approach. The events of time do seem to invite Christian kings to a war in respect of the great corruption and relaxation of discipline in that empire.' It would have been very interesting to us in our day to have been able to read the mature mind of Bacon on the rights and wrongs of a war to be carried on by England and the united West against 'the enemy of Christendom.' But Bacon only lived to overtake a few pages of his *Holy War*. Most happily, however, he had written the preface before he began the body of the book, and he had given to the preface the form of a Dedicatory Letter to Andrewes (now Bishop of Winchester), and a most important piece of Bacon's mental autobiography it is. Dante and Bacon and Milton were three gigantic brothers in intellect, they were each sent into a world wholly out of joint, and they all three write about themselves in their disjointed worlds as only giants are enabled and permitted to write. Bacon's Dedication and Advertisement to his *Holy War* stands beside Dante's classification and comparison of himself with Homer and Virgil, and beside Milton's magnificent proposals and preparations for the work of his life. After comparing his case with the cases of Demosthenes and Cicero and Seneca, Bacon goes on to say to Andrewes this, —'These examples confirmed me in a resolution to spend my time wholly in writing, and to put out that poor talent or half talent, or what it is, that God hath given me, not as heretofore to particular exchanges, but to banks and mounts of perpetuity which will not break. And therefore this work, not for the City, but for the Temple, I have dedicated to your lordship, in respect of ancient and private acquaintance, and because I hold you in special reverence.' Great Bacon, and noble in all his ignobility! 'In his great adversity I prayed,' says

Ben Jonson, 'that God would give him strength, for
greatness he could not want.' 'The most exquisitely
constructed intellect,' says Macaulay, 'that has ever
been bestowed on the children of men.' It is the
fashion to-day to run down Macaulay, but let all
gifted and ambitious young men read that great
writer's Essay on Bacon and lay it to heart once
every year. As for Spedding and Ellis they should
lie beside every young lawyer's Bible and *Private
Devotions*.

There is no finer picture of Andrewes to be seen Casaubon.
anywhere than that which is painted in Mark
Pattison's classical, if somewhat cold and super-
cilious, *Life of Isaac Casaubon*. Though the Rector
of Lincoln says some very severe things of Bishop
Andrewes, at the same time, in no other book that
I know is there such an altogether delightful
glimpse given us of the beauty and attractiveness
of Andrewes's private character. The truly episcopal
hospitality,—his lordship, it was said, kept Christmas
all the year,—the noble courtesy, the exquisite
geniality and tenderness, and the whole gracious-
ness and affectionateness of the bishop's nature
never came out better than all that did in his whole
connection with Casaubon. It is true there were
more things than one that went to attract and to
attach those two men to one another. 'Profound
piety,' says Pattison, 'and great reading, common
to both, placed them at once in sympathy.' But,
besides that, their ecclesiastical views also, their
attitude toward those questions of Church order and
public worship which were agitating and rending all
the churches in Christendom at that day, drew the
scholar and the bishop continually closer and closer
to one another. 'The Anglican ritual,' says his

able biographer, 'exactly met Casaubon's aspirations
after the decent simplicity of primitive worship,
though his Presbyterian sentiment was at first in-
clined to find a little too much pomp and pride
mingling with some parts of the episcopal services.
But, on the whole, he preferred the Anglican
ceremonies to the bare and naked usages of his own
communion. At the same time, he never forsook
the French congregation of which he continued to
be a member. He attended the preaching from
time to time, though not seldom hearing doctrine
from which he differed, and philology which he
knew to be rotten.' But, besides all that, the two
scholars were continually thrown together at Court
in carrying on those loyal labours to which the king
had for so long yoked the bishop, and to assist
the bishop in which with his omnipotent pen the
greatest classical scholar in Europe had been
brought over from France. Chained to his task,
the best ecclesiastical scholar in England had been
toiling for years past at those controversies in which
the Crown and the Church of England had become
involved with the great Catholic theologians and
casuists of that day; and Casaubon's arrival in
London was hailed as the advent of a heaven-sent
assistant to Andrewes and his cause. Long before
they had seen each other's faces Andrewes and
Casaubon were already at one in their intense
hatred of Bellarmine and Baronius, and no sooner
had they shaken hands than they sat down to work
to each other's hands at a task which was to them
at once the service of the Truth, of the Church,
and of the State; the service of God, and of their
king and patron James the First. Casaubon's diary
of those delightful days is full of Andrewes, and

the admiration and the esteem are quite as much,
to his honour be it said, on the great bishop's side
as on the poor scholar's. 'Come and shoot a buck
with me. Throw aside your books this hot weather.
Shut up your Drury Lane lodgings, and let me see
your dear face. I am not well in my solitude, but
a visit from you will set me on my feet. Come
down at once if you would be in time for Stour-
bridge Fair, the finest thing of its kind in all
England. But, if you have no taste for an English
fair, then I have beside me at this moment a
Matthew in Hebrew that will make your mouth
water. Do be persuaded to come. Be so good as
to remember that the hand which writes these lines
is ill with the ague. Coming or going, God keep
you long to be an ornament to letters.' And then
when Casaubon did find his way to the palace at
Downham,—to see the two solitary scholars together is delightful. It is a rebuke and an inspiration to open Casaubon's diary for those holiday
weeks. The two book-lovers read more in the
mornings of their holidays than other men read all
the year round. They breakfasted alone to gain
time and to keep the freshness of the day for their
private devotions and their peculiar studies. And
then they met, the best of company, at their early
mid-day dinner. Andrewes 'doubted,' so Isaacson
reports his master, 'they were no true scholars who
came to speak to a man before noon.' Casaubon was
happy in everything at Ely, the bishop's present
diocese, but in the distance of his books. The bishop
had a fine library, as the catalogue of it still proves;
but, unhappily, it was nearly all in London, where
Andrewes spent the most part of every year in at-
tendance at Court and in writing controversies for the

king. Both Casaubon and Andrewes were of Pericles' mind, and held that not a Greek's best holiday only, but an Englishman's and a Frenchman's best holiday also, was that day on which he did most of his duty. And accordingly the Master of Peterhouse was largely requisitioned for the loan of his most learned books when Andrewes and Casaubon were at Ely. Books and manuscripts were the tools of Casaubon's life, and even if he was not working at his full strength while he was at Ely, at the same time he loved to be feeling the edge of his tools, and to have them and his whetstone always near him. When Casaubon was not composing he was always collecting materials for his next composition. His advice to all true students is this: 'Remember that it is of no use to have read a thing, unless you retain it in your memory. Make notes therefore of everything you read, as aids to your memory.' The books that Casaubon read at Downham and made copious notes of would stagger an ordinary student so much as even to hear their bare names, and he always put at the head of his sheet of notes this motto in Greek, 'Alone and at work with God.' After their mid-day dinner the two friends spent the afternoon walking, riding, visiting the parishes of the diocese, inspecting the church fabrics, entertaining friends, transfixing a buck, but always their best recreation and entertainment was to be talking of books together. Still, with all that, there was nothing that went so deep both into the hearts and into the characters of those two good men as their life of faith, of prayer, and of personal holiness. If there were two saints of God in England that summer, they were surely to be found under the roof of the episcopal palace of Ely. Writing of thirty years before, Pattison's somewhat grudging words are these :—' The religious sentiment was ever suggesting to young Casaubon the futility of worldly knowledge, and the superior value of religious studies. This impression may be traced to the early years of the son of the Huguenot pastor who had to fly to the hills. From the first there were two men in Casaubon, the theologian and the scholar.' And summing up his life, his somewhat too aloof biographer says :—' The habitual attitude of Casaubon's soul was abandonment ; not merely resignation, but prostration before the Unseen. He moved, thought, and felt, as in the presence of God. His family and friends lay near to his heart, but nearer than all is God. In all his thoughts the thought of God is subsumed.' And again, ' his diary is one prolonged litany.' Yes : so it is. David's Psalms were never out of Casaubon's hands, and the best day he spent at Downham was not the day when he transfixed three bucks, but the day when all alone in the bishop's copse he read the Hundred and Nineteenth Psalm over again with a rapturous heart. Pleasantly as his holiday passed, and in spite of the bishop's ' golden chains of courtesy,' Casaubon began to be feverish for London and for his own books. But the great scholar's life of books in this world soon after that came to an end. ' In answer to your questions,' writes Andrewes to Heinsius in 1614, ' regarding the departure of that illustrious man. In the morning of the day on which he died he received the Holy Sacrament from my hand ; and that because three days before he had begged it of me. After the sacrament he expressed a wish that Simeon's Canticle should be chanted. There was nothing in the whole world of the slightest interest to that Christian man Casaubon, unless what related to piety and holiness, and that was most evident amid his last tortures. His remains were buried in Westminster Abbey in front of the doors of that chapel in which the monuments of our kings are seen.'

Summary. Lancelot Andrewes was born of honest and godly parents in 1555. We find him a scholar of Pembroke in 1571, and Dean of Westminster in 1601. Hooker died in 1600 at the age of forty-six, and on hearing of his death Andrewes wrote of him, ' He hath not that I know left any near him.' Queen Elizabeth died in March 1603, and four months later Andrewes assisted at the coronation of James. In 1605 he was raised to be Bishop of Chichester, he was one of the translators of the Bible in 1607, and in 1609 he published his very learned *Tortura Torti* against Cardinal Bellarmine, an uncongenial task, imposed upon him by the king. In the end of the same year he was translated to Ely, where Casaubon spent part of the summer of 1611 with the bishop. In 1613 he sat as one of the judges on the Essex case. In 1617 he attended the king on his visit to Scotland, and in 1618 he was translated from Ely to Winchester. In 1621 Bacon fell, and Andrewes was one of the deputation of peers who attended on Bacon to receive his confession and submission. In 1621 he sat on Archbishop Abbot's case also, and ' the party,' says Thomas Fuller, ' whom the archbishop suspected his greatest foe, proved his most firm and effectual friend, even Lancelot Andrewes, Bishop of Winchester.' In 1625 James died. On his deathbed the king sent for Andrewes, but the favourite Bishop was so ill himself at the time that

it was not possible for him to come to bid his royal
master farewell. On the 2nd of February 1626
Andrewes was able to be present at the coronation
of Charles the First, in which ceremony, both on
account of his high office and his personal accept-
ability, he took a foremost place. This was one of
the last public acts that Andrewes ever performed.
'His gratitude to men,' says his secretary, 'was
now changed into thankfulness to God. His
affability to incessant and devout prayers and
speeches with his Creator and Redeemer and
Sanctifier. His laborious studies to restless groans,
sighs, cries, and tears. His hands labouring, his
eyes lifted up, and his heart beating and panting to
see the living God, even to the last of his breath.'
Under Monday the 25th of September 1626 we read
in Archbishop Laud's diary this entry : 'About four
o'clock in the morning died Lancelot Andrewes,
the most worthy Bishop of Winchester, the great
light of the Christian world.' Andrewes has left
behind him five volumes of sermons, preached for
the most part at Court, and on special occasions ;
two or three volumes of controversial matter, a
volume of catechetical matter, and the *Private
Devotions*. The *Private Devotions*, as the name
indicates, was never intended for publication.
Andrewes wrote the little book for his own use,
and then, when he was done with it, he gave it to
his great friend Archbishop Laud.

AN INTERPRETATION

The Psalter.

THE Book of Psalms is by far the oldest and it is by far the best of all the books of public or of private devotion that we possess. The Book of Psalms is the model also as it is the mother of all the excellent books of devotion that we possess in addition to itself. In the Early Church and in the Latin Church of the middle ages a great body of liturgical and other devotional matter grew up and lay scattered about throughout Western Christendom of which the Roman Breviary is a compilation and a condensation,—its own name and title tell us as much. And taken as a whole,—in its immense size and in its very real riches, as well as in its military-like order and method and dramatic movement,—with all its grave and obvious faults, the Roman Breviary is not wholly unworthy of its great name. And then the Book of Common Prayer is just a purer and a more portable English Church Breviary. The Bible, the Breviary, and the ancient liturgies, both Greek and Latin and Anglo-Saxon, were the authoritative and acknowledged sources out of which the Book of Common Prayer was compiled at first, and time after time improved. In the first edition of Bishop Sparrow's Rationale of the Book of Common Prayer there is an old print representing

The Breviary.

The English Prayer-Book.

the twelve compilers of the English Prayer-Book sitting at work around a table. At the head of the learned company Archbishop Cranmer is seen with his hand on an open Bible. Bishop Ridley sits at Cranmer's right hand with the Fathers open before him, and on the archbishop's other side Bishop Goodrich sits with the ancient Liturgies spread open. 'These learned Bishops and Divines,' says Downes in his preface to Sparrow, 'proceeded to inspect and examine the missals, breviaries, rituals, pontificals, graduals, psalters, antiphonals, and all other service-books then in use.'

The Eastern Churches have a very noble devotional literature, which has been made accessible to the English student in the works of Maskell, Palmer, Neale, Littledale, Hammond, Bright, and Robertson, as well as in the Prayer-Books of Edward and Elizabeth. And such heirs of such riches are we, and such joint-heirs with all the Churches, that we possess yet another great treasure in the more private and more personal devotional books of all ages and all nations. We have the Confessions of Augustine, the Prayers and Soliloquies of Anselm, the unfinished Holy Week and other great prayers and praises of Jacob Behmen, the Golden Grove of Jeremy Taylor, the Private Devotions of Lancelot Andrewes, and William Laud, and Thomas Wilson, and many other suchlike precious possessions. But, for its peculiar purpose and for its special use, Andrewes's *Private Devotions* stands out at the head of them all. There is nothing in the whole range of devotional literature to be set beside Andrewes's incomparable *Devotions*. Its author's public and private life; his intense conscience of his past sins and of his abiding sinfulness; his

The *Private Devotions*.

keen, all-realising faith in God and in the grace
of God; his soaring and adoring love; his universal
scholarship, especially in the sacred schools; his
so original method and so peculiar plan in the conception and in the composition of his book; and
the long lifetime of profoundest penitential and
importunate prayer that he has put into his book,—
all these and many other things combine to make
Bishop Andrewes's *Private Devotions* to stand alone
and unapproached in the literature of the closet
and the mercy-seat. To myself one of the chiefest
compensations and off-sets for the reign of James
the First is this, that the *Private Devotions* of
Lancelot Andrewes were being continually composed and were being continually employed,—
were being continually wrung out of him,—
during the whole course of that so mischievous
and insufferable reign. As the chief interest of
the reign of this and that king of Judah and
Israel lies in such and such prophets and psalmists
and righteous men who lived and wrote in the
reigns of those kings, so is it with us in our own
national history. Kings and queens, protectors
and presidents, and the times of their rule, are
ultimately memorable and honourable still by
nothing so much as by the good and the great men
they had among their subjects, the progress that
the Kingdom of Heaven made in their day, and
not least by the number and the quality of the
books belonging to the Kingdom of Heaven that
were written in their day. And that the English
Bible, the Five Sermons on the Sacraments, Donne's
Sermons, and the *Private Devotions*—not to speak in
this place of *Macbeth,* and *Hamlet,* and *Lear,* and the
Essays, and the *Advancement*—have all come down to

us out of James's day, that covers a multitude of the sins of his day, and that will make his day to remain rich and illustrious to all time in the estimation of the Church of Christ in our land, and in all other English-reading lands. It is to James's insight that we owe it that John Donne ever was a minister,—of whom Professor Saintsbury says that in the strength and savour of his quality he has no rival in English, no rival indeed anywhere but in the author of the *Confessions.*

I shall not take time to enter on the Bibliography Biblio-of the *Private Devotions.* I shall not stay to tell graphy. how in 1648, twenty-two years after Andrewes's death, Richard Drake published a translation of the *Devotions* 'out of a fair Greek manuscript of the bishop's amanuensis': how the Greek original on which Richard Drake worked was printed at the Oxford University Press in 1675: how Stanhope, and Hall, and Newman, and Neale, and Venables have all followed Drake with their own translations and transcripts of the *Devotions*: how at Newman's hands 'the *Devotions,*' to borrow Dean Church's words, 'has received in our own times one of those rare translations which make an old book new': and how, by a fortunate purchase, Mr Livingstone of Pembroke College, Oxford, came into the possession of a small manuscript volume, bound in white vellum much discoloured, and tied with four strings of green silk ribbon, on the cover of which the faded inscription is still to be read—*My reverend Friend Bishop Andrewes gave me this Booke a little before his death. W: Bath et Welles.* 'Had you seen the original manuscript,' writes Drake, 'happy in the glorious deformity thereof, being slubbered with its author's pious hands and watered with

his penitential tears, you would have been forced
to confess, that book belonged to no other than
to pure and primitive devotion.' Canon Medd
has published a careful edition of this precious
relic, and we only wait now for another Newman
to arise and to put it into fit and final English
for us.

Method of
Composi-
tion.

In the composition of his *Devotions*, Lancelot
Andrewes had anticipated and had already fulfilled
all William Law's best counsels. 'When at any
time,' Law advises us, 'either in reading the Scrip-
tures or any book of piety, you meet with a passage
that more than ordinarily affects your mind, and
seems as it were to give your heart a new motion
toward God, you should try to turn it into the form
of a petition, and then give it a place in your
prayers. By this means you would be often im-
proving your prayers, and storing yourself with
proper forms of making the desires of your heart
known unto God.' And, again, returning in
another place to the same subject : 'if they were
to collect the best forms of devotion, and to use
themselves to transcribe the finest passages of
Scripture-prayers ; if they were to collect the
devotions, confessions, petitions, praises, resigna-
tions, and thanksgivings, which are scattered up
and down the Psalms, and range them under
proper heads, as so much proper fuel for the flame
of their own devotions; if their minds were often
thus employed, sometimes meditating upon them,
sometimes getting them by heart, and making
them habitual as their own thoughts, how fervently
would they pray, who came thus prepared to pray !'
Now, this was exactly and to the letter what
Andrewes had already done a hundred years to a

day before Law so pleaded with his readers. When Andrewes met with a verse or a clause or so much as a word in any scripture that specially suited into his own case; when David, or Asaph, or Job, or Paul said anything, or hinted at anything, that went to Andrewes's heart, on the spot he took that word down, and that too in its own native Hebrew or Greek, as the case might be. And he did the same thing when he would be reading any of the ancients of the Latin or Orient Kirks, as Robert Bruce called them. Such is the labour of those who write the masterpieces in any branch of letters. Andrewes made such a constant practice of this, and had formed such a settled habit of it, that as his life went on his book of secret prayer came to be filled with all the best passages in the Psalms, in the Prophets, in the Gospels, and in the Epistles, as also in the sermons and litanies and liturgies of the Fathers and the Saints, till we have a perfect portrait before us of Andrewes's inmost soul, and that too in lines and in colours borrowed from those hands which could best draw such deep lines and best mix such strong and lasting colours. Every verse, every clause of a verse, every single word and syllable, indeed, that Andrewes quotes has some special and inspired reference to himself alone. It is not quotation with him, it is assimilation; it is appropriation; and it is the recovery and the re-appropriation of that which is indisputably his own wherever he comes across it. He passes over whole chapters and whole books in silence and with a dry pen. Only this one word in this whole Psalm is his, and he straightway takes this one word out of the whole Psalm and leaves to its author and to its other readers all the rest of the Psalm. He takes but what is demonstrably his own, and what has no such interest and no such value to any one else, and he hides it ever afterwards in his heart. He steals it down from all eyes into the book which he never opens till after his door is shut. And thus it is that all formality, all insincerity, all mere lip-service, and all multiplying of sacred words for the sake of their sound is excluded from this severe, sincere, and serious little book. The author's method with himself and with his Bible excludes all that, and protects him and his readers from their constant temptation to all that.

Andrewes carried out the same method of selection and assimilation as he read the devotional books of the Greek and the Latin Fathers. Only, I feel sure that a great deal too much has been made of what Andrewes owes to the Greek and the Latin litanists and liturgists. Now and then you will come on a passage that is plainly borrowed from Chrysostom, or Basil, or the 'Liturgy of St. James,' but for one word that Andrewes owes to Chrysostom he owes a hundred to David. The truth is, the *Devotions* are far more original, so to call it, than has ever been allowed even by those who are tempted to sacrifice the plain truth to their partiality and their praise of Andrewes. All that Mozley says so uncritically and so extravagantly about Andrewes's sermons, with some chastening and some selecting, could then be very well and very truly said about his *Devotions*. And I venture to prophesy that when the genuine and original Laudian text has been translated, and when all the scriptural and liturgical and other quotations, references, and allusions have been traced up to their sources, the bishop's book will nevertheless be seen to be absolutely his own.

The main sources from which he drew were the
Holy Scriptures and his own life. The *Institutiones
Piæ* is a little volume of clear, simple, sweet English
writing, not at all equal in depth or in strength to
the *Devotions*, but a great improvement on the style
of the sermons. This and the *Manual for the Sick*
are excellent little books, and were the product
of Andrewes's personal religion and of his pastoral
work when he was as yet an obscure and a single-
hearted young minister with his whole time and
his whole strength given up to his pulpit and to
his pastorate.

To the question why the best part of the *Devotions* Why in
was written in Greek, I have no better answer to Greek?
offer than that which honest Stationer Moseley
offered to the Christian reader from his shop in
St. Paul's Churchyard in 1647. 'He penned them
in Greek, and in that language presented them to
his God; the reason is not for me to determine;
whether it were for that the evidences of our
salvation are delivered to us in that tongue, or
whether amongst those fifteen he was master of,
he chose this language as the most copious to
express the fulness of his soul.' To which let me
add this out of the Preface to Dean Stanhope's
translation : 'Such of his prayers as were brought
nearest to perfection he wrote in Greek, either
because the New Testament, the Septuagint, and
most of the ancient Fathers and Liturgies, whence
he extracted a good deal, were in that language, or
because that language had some advantage for
devotion, as the many compound words it contains
strengthen the ideas they convey to us, and make
a more lively impression on the mind.' The fulness
of the Greek spirit also, in its form, order, elevation,

taste, beauty, music, falls on Andrewes, and for the
first time takes full possession of Andrewes, when
he enters his closet. And thus it is that, when we
take Andrewes's method and manner of composition along with his sources and with the language
he wrote in, we have before us in his *Private
Devotions* a perfect portrait of that man of prayer.
We have Andrewes, in his *Devotions,* if not altogether
as God saw him, at any rate as he saw himself when
he felt himself to be more immediately under the eye
of God. And thus it is that it is not David we see
even in the most Davidic of Andrewes's prayers, nor
Asaph in the most Asaphic of them, nor Paul nor
James nor Chrysostom : but what we see there is
what was true of Andrewes in them all, with something added that was in none of them all, and is
in no one else but in Lancelot Andrewes in all the
world.

His Week
of Prayer.

The First Chapter of Genesis supplies to Andrewes
the mould and the framework upon which he shapes
and constructs his book, and a right noble use he
makes of the majestic movement and the splendid
scenery of that superb chapter. With that superb
and splendid chapter open before him, Andrewes
addresses himself to prepare a week of prayer and
praise somewhat corresponding to the week of
creation. And he opens and begins each successive
day of his devotional week with an entranced and
adoring meditation on the divine work of each successive day, as that divine work is described to him in
the opening chapter of the Book of Genesis. And
God said, Let there be light : and there was light.
And God saw the light, that it was good : and God
divided the light from the darkness. And God
called the light Day, and the darkness He called

The First
Day.

Night. Andrewes reads that on the morning of the First Day. He tarries over what he reads. He meditates upon it. He is present at it. He sees it. He hears it. And or ever he is aware his heart has burst out of him with this adoration,— Glory be to Thee, O Lord. Glory be to Thee, Thou Creator of the light, Thou Enlightener of the world. Creator of the visible light, the sun's radiance, the flame of fire. Creator also of the light invisible and intellectual,—the revelation of God, the writings of the holy law, the oracles of sacred prophecy, the music of sacred psalmody, the instruction of the sapiential books, and the experience of Scripture history—on all of which a light shines which shall see no night. As it is sung every First Day of the Week in the Roman Breviary:

> Father of Lights, by whom each day
>   Is kindled out of night,
> Who, when the heavens were made, didst lay
>   Their rudiments in light.
> Thou, who didst bind and blend in one
>   The glistening morn and evening pale,
> Hear Thou our plaint, when light is gone,
>   And lawlessness and strife prevail.

In his magnificent adoration for the First Day Andrewes is above himself. On the First Day he stands beside Hooker and Milton. Here Andrewes is as good as Hooker is at his seraphic best. This is Hooker's immortal First Book set to temple music. This is Bacon also in his great prayer after his fall: in that great prayer of which Addison says that it is the devotion of an angel rather than a man. 'Thy creatures have been my book, but thy scriptures much more. I have sought Thee in the courts, in the fields, and in the garden, but I have found Thee in Thy holy temple.' Andrewes's First Day will always be written on the margin of the First Chapter of Genesis and on the margin of the Nineteenth Psalm in my Bible.

The Second Day. On the morning of the Second Day Andrewes opens Moses again. Let there be a firmament in the midst of the waters, and let it divide the waters from the waters : and it was so. And as he reads and sees what he reads, he recollects what he had seen written in the 'divine liturgy of St. Clement,' and he turns to the ancient devotional writer and thus meditates with him and thus prays with him : 'My voice shalt Thou hear in the morning, O Lord. Blessed art Thou Who didst create the firmament of heaven, and the powers of the intellectual heaven, the angels, the archangels, the cherubim, and the seraphim : the waters above the heavens, mists and vapours, for showers, dew, snow as wool, hoar frost as ashes, ice as morsels, clouds from the ends of the earth, winds and waters out of Thy treasuries and out of Thy chambers.' And then the liturgy continues: 'Thou didst establish the great deep also, and didst cast a mound of sea-shore round about it, till a world of salt water stands up as an heap bounded on every side with Thy great barriers of rock and sand. Sometimes Thou dost swell the sea with a wind so as to lift it up into great mountains, and sometimes Thou dost smooth it out into a plain for the ease and the delight of mariners.' And after much more of that same elevated and eloquent kind, all the people answer in a chant: 'Holy, holy, holy, is the Lord of Sabaoth : the heavens, and the earth, and the seas are all full to us of His glory. Blessed be the name of the Lord for evermore. Amen.'

And on the Third Day God said, Let the earth The Third Day. bring forth grass, the herb yielding seed, and the fruit tree yielding fruit, whose seed is in itself: and it was so: and God saw that it was good. And straightway Andrewes sees all creation with a sacramental eye, in the light and in the unction of which he sings, 'O God, Thou art my God. Blessed art Thou, O Lord, who gatheredst the water into the sea, and broughtest to sight the earth, and madest to sprout all herbs and all fruit-bearing trees. There at Thy word are the oceans and the seas with their lakes and rivers and fountains. There also are the mountains, the hills, and the vales; glebe lands, meadow lands, and glades; there are pastures, and corn fields, and grass for cattle; herbs for food and for medicine; flowers for beauty; and fruit trees, and vines, and olive trees, and spices; trees for timber also, and stones for building, and metals for all arts, and coal, and fire, and vapour of smoke.'

And then on the morning of the Fourth Day The Fourth Day. Andrewes offers this adoration: I have meditated on thee, O Lord, in the night watches, for Thou hast been my help. Or as it is in a Breviary Matin:

> Be Thou the first on every tongue,
>   The first in every heart;
> That all our doings all day long,
>   Holiest! may from Thee start.

Blessed art Thou, O Lord, Who madest the two great lights, sun and moon, and the stars also, for light, for signs, and for seasons: for spring, summer, autumn, winter: for days, and weeks, and months, and years. The sun to rule the day and the moon to rule the night. 'O Lord,' so runs the Breviary Hymn for Wednesday, a hymn which has received one of those rare translations that make an old hymn new :

> Who didst on the Fourth Day, in heaven,
> Light the fierce cresset of the sun,
>   And the meek moon at even,
>   And stars that wildly run ;
>
> That they might mark and arbitrate
> 'Twixt alternating night and day,
>   And tend the train sedate
>   Of months upon their way ;
>
> Clear, Lord, the brooding night within,
> And cleanse these hearts for thy abode,
>   Unlock the spell of sin,
>   Crumble its giant load.

The Fifth Day.

'Thursday, next to Sunday,' says Dr Cazenove in a valuable paper of memoranda that my revered friend has favoured me with, 'is the most jubilant day of the week. There is the intense triumph of our fallen nature having been renewed and exalted in the person of the ascended Lord above all angels and archangels to the right hand of the Father. Moreover, it is the day of the institution of the sacred feast of Holy Communion. Christ's advocacy for us, the graces taught in the beatitudes, the gifts bestowed upon His saints, especially upon His holy mother, are blended with intercessions, and that day's prayer is concluded with a wonderful list of thanksgivings.'

The Sixth Day.

And God said, Let us make man in our image, after our likeness : so God created man in His own image, in the image of God created He him : male and female created He them. I have always thought Andrewes's extraordinarily compressed meditation on that passage to be one of his finest things. In a few noble words he rises to the full height of Moses' great argument : ' In the

morning shall my prayer prevent Thee. Blessed art
Thou, O Lord, Who broughtest forth the beasts of
the earth, and cattle, and creeping things, for food,
for the clothing and for the assistance of man. And
then Thou madest man himself after Thine own
image, and blessedst him, and didst put all things
under his feet. The fore-counsel concerning man ;
the hand that fashioned him ; the image of God
within him ; the putting of all things under him ;
and the charge to the angels to guard him, to
cherish him, and to minister to him. His heart,
his reins, his eyes, his ears, his tongue, his hands,
his feet, his life, his reason, his spirit, his free will,
his memory, his conscience, the revelation of God
made to him, the written law put into his hands,
oracles of prophets also, melody of psalms, instruction of proverbs, experience of histories, worship and
sacrifice. Blessed art Thou also for Thy great and
precious promise made on this day concerning the
life-giving seed, and for the fulfilment of that
promise in the fulness of time on this day.'

And then under each successive day of creation, Heads of
and after the proper meditation and adoration for Devotion.
the day, there comes a series of devotions arranged
under the five heads of Confession of sin, Prayer
for mercy to pardon and grace to help, Confession
of faith, Intercession, and Thanksgiving ; 'so universal,' as Stationer Moseley says, 'was Lancelot
Andrewes in all holy dimensions.' Every day of
his holy week begins with a meditation and an
adoration on the creation of the world till all
creation is crowned on the sixth day with the
creation of man. And then immediately after each
day's proper meditation there follows a most Confession
poignant confession of sin : 'They continue this of Sin.

day according to Thine ordinances: for all are Thy servants. But,' adds Andrewes, 'I have destroyed myself. For, two things I ever see in myself, human nature which Thou hast made in Thine own image, and my sin by which I have depraved and destroyed myself. My sin and my self-destruction are new again every morning before me.' Scripture completely 'disables our nature,' as Andrewes says in his first sermon on Prayer, and the *Devotions* follows hard after Scripture in that. Andrewes confessed every morning with Bacon, 'thousand have been my sins, and ten thousand my transgressions. As Thy favours have increased upon me, so have Thy corrections; and ever as my worldly blessings were exalted, so secret darts from Thee have pierced me, and when I have ascended before men, I have descended in humiliation before Thee.' When Hacket praised Andrewes for his extraordinary kindness and attention to the students of Westminster, their old dean only the more remembered the many young men of promise who had gone astray owing to his forgetfulness and neglect. He had taught them to read and to write in Latin and in Greek, but he had overlooked to teach them to pray and to know themselves. When Bacon fell, and when Andrewes had to sit in judgment upon the Lord Chancellor's distractingly sad case, he remembered how that great man had been used to call him his inquisitor, but Andrewes had secret remorse to the day of his death that he had not early enough and often enough been Bacon's intercessor. When men talked everywhere of his hospitality and of his bountifulness, Andrewes remembered how much of that of which he was only the steward he had

spent upon himself, and how much upon masks
and feasts and progresses to his over-feasted, over-
amused, and over-flattered king. And as scandal
after scandal leaped to light out of the wide-spread
corruption and crime of the Essex case, Andrewes
took all the condemnation of that miserable case
home to himself. Had I acted like Abbot I should
certainly have shared with Abbot in the hatred and
the revenge of the king and the court, but I
should have stopped that dreadful crime, and I
should have saved the souls of all concerned in it.
Who can understand the reach and the longevity
of his errors? Andrewes cried out all his days,
Against Thee, Thee only, have I sinned! There is
nothing that has ever been felt by any of God's
saints that Andrewes feels so much as that he is
the chief of sinners. Paul must have felt that, else
he would never have said it. Bunyan also must
have felt it, else he would never have penned the
title-page of his *Grace Abounding*. But Andrewes's
Devotions convinces me that he felt that as much as
any great saint of God of them all. There is
something about the way that Andrewes says it
that makes me believe what he says, out to the
uttermost stretch and strain of it. 'God be
merciful to me a sinner, the chief of sinners. . . .
Lord be merciful to me a sinner, even unto me,
O Lord, of sinners chief, chiefest and greatest. . . .
The just man falleth seven times a day, and I, an
exceeding sinner, seventy times seven, a fearful
and a horrible thing, O Lord. Thine unspeakable and unimaginable goodness, and Thy pity
toward sinners and unworthy, and toward me of
all sinners far the most unworthy,—an unworthy,
wretched, and abject sinner. . . . Be merciful to

me a sinner, be merciful to me of all sinners the
greatest and the most wretched. . . . Have mercy
on me a sinner, the greatest of sinners, and for
that very reason in need of the greatest mercy. . . .
I then, trusting in Thy mercy, that forgiveth at the
least seventy times seven, stand afar off, and bowed
to the very dust I say again and again, God have
mercy on me a sinner, on me a most wretched
sinner, on me the chief of sinners, on me who am
altogether made of sin, on me, who am a very
hyperbole of sin.' There is no doubt about
language like that. That is not imitation. That
is not repetition. That is not so many words. That
is the very sacrifice with which God is well pleased.
With that man will I dwell, saith the Lord, wherever
he sees or hears the like of that. You would think
that was surely enough. But no. The grave, and
the two daughters of the horseleech, may say, That
it is enough; but not Bishop Andrewes's sinful
heart. 'I need more grief,' he cries. 'I plainly
need more grief. I am far from that grief which I
ought to have. I can sin much, but I cannot
repent much. O my dryness and my deadness!
Woe unto me! Would that I had more grief and
sorrow of heart. But of myself I cannot obtain it.
I am dried up like a potsherd. Open in me, O
Lord, a fountain of tears. Give me a molten heart.
. . . I despise and bruise myself that my penitence,
O Lord, is not deeper, is not fuller. Help Thou
mine impenitence, and more, and still more pierce
Thou, rend, and crush my heart. I am a burden
to myself in that I cannot sorrow more. I beseech
from Thee therefore a contrite heart, groanings that
cannot be uttered, tears of blood. More and more
bruise, and wound, and pierce, and strike my heart.

Thou canst turn even the hard rock into a pool.
Give tears then: give the grace of tears. Give me,
O Lord, this great grace. Tears such as Thou didst
give to David, to Jeremiah, to Peter, and to Mary
Magdalene.' 'Tears gain everything,' says Santa
Teresa in her Autobiography, and Andrewes would
seem to have been of her belief. And because he
had such sin, so much sin, and so little sorrow for so
much sin, he cursed himself, he spat in his own face,
and he cast himself into the ditch. 'Despise me
not utterly, O God, who am an unclean worm, a
dead dog, a body of death.' You will remember the
prayer that was found in William Law's handwriting
among his papers: 'Sanctify, O Lord, I beseech
thee, this punishment to the benefit of my soul.
That by Thy blessing it may heal my sores, take
out the stains, deliver me from the shame, and
rescue me from the tyranny of sin. But, O my God,
I am an unclean worm, a dead dog, a stinking car-
case, justly removed from that society of saints who
this day kneel about thine altars. Let me be
blessed and sanctified, as thou blessest and sancti-
fiest those that lament in sackcloth and ashes.'
Lancelot Andrewes and William Law would seem
to have been well read in the Missal of Matthias
Illyricus; or rather, all three were well read in
their Bible.

There is a very remarkable argument carried on
in the early part of the Eighty-sixth Tract for the
Times,—a Tract which could only have been written
by one of two men. And the argument is to the
effect that the Reformation was the outcome of a
universal call to repentance on the part of God, and
that on the part of the Church of England it was
a response to that call in a great act of national

humiliation and sorrow for sin. And the subtle and skilful writer of the Tract, having taken that thesis in hand, goes on to trace the proof of that and the effect of that in the changes made in the Collects of the English Prayer-Book at the time of the Reformation. And he points out what he calls a lowering of the voice, a descent of the mind, and a humbling of the heart of the Church from the high choral tone of the missals and the breviaries and the early liturgies, till the Book of Common Prayer has become the cry of a returning prodigal rather than an expression of the liberty and the joy of obedient children. And it cannot be denied that Bishop Andrewes is a true son of the English Church in this respect. He is at his best in repentance and confession. He prays and praises in many places like a son also. But like volcanic rock thrusting itself up through a harvest field, so does Andrewes's acute and abiding remorse for sin pierce up through his finest and fullest psalms of thanksgiving. Andrewes comes again with rejoicing, bringing his sheaves with him, but all his harvest field has been sown in tears, and so reaped, and so gathered in, and so garnered, till it is the bread of tears. 'His piety has not softened his heart,' says Mark Pattison in a cruel and revengeful passage. But Andrewes would have said with John Foxe that what his piety had not done his impiety had completely accomplished. I owe far more to my sins, says the old martyrologist, than I owe to my good works. Andrewes has three Acts of Confession in his Latin Devotions, and all three are out of the same still broken heart. But the second of the three, beginning with—'O God, Thou knowest my foolishness,'—it exceeds. I shall not touch it. I shall not attempt to give examples out of it. The page would run blood if I broke off a single sentence of it. Only, if ever God got at the hands of a sinful man a sacrifice that satisfied Him and made Him say on the spot, Bring forth the best robe, it was surely in Lancelot Andrewes's closet, and after that great Act of Confession.

One of the acknowledged masters of the spiritual life warns us against 'an untheological devotion. True spirituality,' he insists, ' has always been ortho-dox.' And the readers of the *Grammar of Assent* Confession will remember with what masterly power and with of Faith. what equal eloquence it is there set forth that the theology of the Creeds and of the Catechisms, when it is rightly understood and properly employed, appeals to the heart quite as much as to the head, to the imagination quite as much as to the understanding. And we cannot study Andrewes's book, his closet confession of his faith especially, without discovering what a majesty, what a massiveness, what a depth, and what a strength, as well as what an evangelical fervour and heartsomeness his theology has given to his devo-tional life. Take in illustration this profound apos-trophe—the sum of so much that is contained in the *Devotions* : ' Essence beyond essence : Essence every-where, and wholly everywhere !' Let the intellect and the imagination take that of God truly, fully, and long enough up, and forthwith Andrewes's words will take rank not unworthily with John's words, 'No man hath seen God at any time,' and with Paul's words, ' Dwelling in the light which no man can approach unto.' To some minds those three words in which Andrewes describes the Divine Nature will flash a new light on many an old expression of the Scrip-tures and the Catechisms and the Creeds. Let any

devout and thoughtful man take up Andrewes's confession of faith for the Fourth Day imaginatively and
affectionately, and let each strong heaven-laden word
be meditated and prayed over, and he will experience
in himself what is meant by the power and the pro-
fitableness of a theological devotion. 'I believe
in the Father's lovingkindness; in the Almighty's
saving power; in the Creator's providence for
guarding, ruling, perfecting the universe; in Jesus,
for salvation; in Christ, for the anointing of his Holy
Spirit; in the only begotten Son, for adoption; in
the Lord, for His care as our Master; in his conception and birth, for the cleansing of our unclean
conception and birth; in His sufferings, endured that
we, whose due they were, might not suffer; in His
cross, for the curse of the law removed; in His death,
for the sting of death taken away; in His descent
whither we ought, that we might not go; in His resurrection, as the first fruits of them that sleep; in
His ascension, to prepare a place for us; in His sitting,
to appear and to intercede for us; in His return, to
take unto Him His own; in His judgment, to
render to every man according to his deeds; in the
Holy Ghost, for power from on high, transform-
ing unto sanctity from without and invisibly, yet
effectually and evidently; in the Church, a body
mystical of those called out of the whole world into
a commonwealth of faith and holiness; in the communion of saints, members of this body, a partaking
with one another of holy things, for assurance of the
remission of sins, for hope of resurrection and translation to life everlasting.' In the *Grammar of Assent*
its author says that for himself he has ever felt the
Athanasian Creed to be the most devotional formulary
to which Christianity has given birth. We certainly

feel something not unlike that when Andrewes
takes up the Apostles' Creed, or the Nicene Creed,
or the Life of our Lord, or His Names, or His Titles,
or His Attributes, or His Offices.   When Andrewes
takes up any of these things into his intellect, imagination, and heart, he has already provided himself and
his readers with another great prayer and another
great psalm.   So true is it that all true theology is
directly and richly and evangelically devotional.

No one can have any idea of the power and the Interces-
beauty, the breadth and at the same time the par- sion.
ticularity of Andrewes's intercessions, who has not
for long made use of them as the coal of this so much
neglected altar in his own devotional life.   William
Law is always insisting on particulars, and instances,
and specifications ; on names of people, names of
places, and names of things in all prayer, and
especially in intercessory prayer.   And, even with
Law himself open before me, I know no master of
instances and particulars in intercessory prayer like
Andrewes.   Those who have not discovered the
Devotions have a great start forward still before
them when they begin to make constant use of that
great book.   I shall rejoice if these weak words of
mine shall succeed in persuading even one man to
take Andrewes for his teacher and his pattern in
his life of intercessory prayer.

And then his thanksgivings.   Read them, sing Thanks-
them, carry them about with you, drink in their giving
spirit, and offer your own thanksgivings on their
noble plan.   The Thanksgiving for the Fifth Day
is an absolutely unique piece of sacred song.   It is
an all-embracing, absolutely exhaustive, autobio-
graphic psalm.   It is written by a man of God for
God alone to read and to hear.   And as we are

chosen and privileged to read it and to hear it we come to understand something of the secret life of a man who was said to spend five hours of the day sometimes over a prayer and a psalm. We ourselves will spend as many hours, and we will not be done with our praise, when we have learned Andrewes's divine art of writing and reading our own autobiography to God. 'O God, for my existence, my life, my reason; for nurture, protection, guidance, education, civil rights, religion; for thy gifts to me of grace, nature, worldly good; for redemption, regeneration, instruction in the truth; for my call, recall, yea, many calls all through life; for Thy forbearance, longsuffering, long longsuffering toward me, even until now; for all good things received, for all successes granted to me, for all good deeds I have been enabled to do; for my parents honest and good, for teachers kind, for benefactors never to be forgotten, for religious intimates so congenial and so helpful, for hearers thoughtful, friends true and sincere, servants faithful; for all who have helped me by their writings, sermons, conversations, prayers, examples, rebukes, and even injuries; for all these, and for all others which I know, and which I know not, open, hidden, remembered, forgotten;—what shall I render unto the Lord for all His benefits?' And, then, on an altogether other key, An Act of Thanksgiving in the Latin Part. 'If I were compelled to make a choice,' says Dr Cazenove, 'I should select the Act of Thanksgiving.' Before I knew Dr Cazenove's choice, I find I had already spoken of it as 'that magnificent Act of Thanksgiving. Surely the noblest service of that kind that ever rose from earth to heaven. Yes, it is wholly worthy to be taken up word for word by the great multitude that no man can number. They cannot sing a better song. It is in every word of it worthy of them and of the place where they stand.' And if any man think that too much to say about a book whose very title he has never heard till to-night, let him begin from to-night to learn to thank God with Lancelot Andrewes. Those who are staggered and offended to be told that any man should spend hours upon hours alone with himself and with his Maker should study such prayers and psalms as those of Andrewes; and if they once enter into their genius, and come under their spell, they will have discovered a new way of redeeming and laying out the dregs of their days.

In trying to account for Andrewes having composed the most finished parts of his *Devotions* in Greek, Mr. Hutton, Dean Stanhope's editor, says that the compound and emphatic words of that language greatly strengthen the ideas they convey to us, and thus make a deeper impression on our minds. Now no adequate justice can at all be done to Andrewes's *Devotions* till attention has been called to the power and the impressiveness of some of his single words and short sentences. The weight, the concentration, the solidity, and the impact of the style is one of the foremost features of Andrewes's *Devotions*. I have never forgotten the impression that one word of his in one of his confessions of sin made on my own imagination and heart the first time it leaped out upon me. 'I have neglected thee, O God!' Andrewes cried, and I trembled as I heard him cry it. And I have never come upon that awful word from that day to this without a shudder. That I should neglect God! A man who has all his life neglected God,—Andrewes has

Single words and short sentences.

'I have neglected Thee.'

made me see that to be my true description. If I make
my bed in hell at last Andrewes has made me hear
them pointing me out and saying, That is the man
lying there who neglected God! It is this neglect
of God that makes so many men infidels and atheists
and outcasts. You neglect God till you come to
say, and that not without some reason, that there
simply cannot be such and such a God else it would
be a sheer impossibility that you could have neglected
Him as you have done. You look within, and you
look around, and you see yourself and all men
absolutely pushing God aside till it is as good as
demonstrated to you that there can be no God.
'God,' said John Donne in a sermon that Andrewes
may very well have heard, 'God is like us in this
also, that He takes it worse to be slighted, to be
neglected, to be left out, than to be actually in-
jured. Our inconsideration, our not thinking of
God in our actions, offends him more than our sins.'
'Pardon,' cries Bishop Wilson in his *Sacra Privata*,
'that I have passed so many days without admiring,
without acknowledging and confessing Thy wonderful goodness to the most unworthy of Thy servants.
Preserve in my soul, O God, such a constant and
clear sense of my obligations to Thee, that upon
every new receipt of Thy favour, I may immediately
turn my eyes to Him from Whom cometh my salvation.' And in an evening prayer that Andrewes
draws out for a family, in the *Institutiones Piæ*,
he makes them all say, 'We have fled from Thee
seeking us: neglected Thee loving us: stopped our
ears to Thee speaking to us: turned our backs to
Thee reaching Thy hand to us: forgotten Thee
doing good to us: and despised Thee correcting us.'
And then in the *Manual for the Sick* he makes the

dying man say,—'I have not studied to seek and
know Thee as I ought to do. Knowing Thee, I
have not glorified Thee, nor given thanks to Thee
accordingly.' And again when Andrewes cries in
another confession,—'I have withstood Thee, O
God,' that makes almost as terrible an impression
on my mind, as well it may. 'I will confess my
iniquity, for I have transgressed, and neglected
Thee, O Lord. Set not my misdeeds before Thee,
nor my life in the light of Thy countenance. I
have withstood Thee, Lord, but I return unto Thee.
I take with me words, and I return unto Thee
and say, Take away all iniquity, and receive me
graciously.' And still, after all that, we see Andrewes
still struggling with some 'relics of reluctancy,' to
the end of his seraphic old age.

'I am made of sin,' Andrewes cries out in one of
his great acts of confession. 'I have sinned, and
of a truth I am made of sin, and my whole life
maketh it manifest.' Only those out of whose
broken heart the echo comes : And so am I !—only
they will believe that Bishop Andrewes can be in
honest earnest and in his sound senses when he
says that. But they who feel that to be true of
themselves,—literally and absolutely true and far
short of the truth,—they will be drawn irresistibly
to the man who first made such a discovery as that
in himself, and who had the truth and the talent
to put the discovery into such answering words.
Andrewes belongs to the family of Abraham, and
Isaiah, and Paul, and Neri, and Pascal, and Bunyan,
and Law, and all the evangelical succession. 'I am
made of dust and ashes,' Abraham said. 'From
the head to the foot I am made up of putrefying
sores,' said Isaiah. 'In me there dwelleth no good

I am made
of sin.'

thing,' said Paul. 'Begone, I am a devil, and not a man,' said Philip. 'I defy the devil himself to equal me,' said the author of *Grace Abounding*. 'We are made up of falsehood, duplicity, and insincerity,' said Pascal, 'and we cloak up these things in ourselves from ourselves.' 'Man is only a compound of corrupt and disorderly tempers,' says William Law. 'I am made of sin,' groans Andrewes, and with that one awful word he lets us down into the whole bottomless pit of sin and shame and pain and misery that is in his own evil heart. 'I am a burden to myself,' he continues, still on his face before God, 'I am a ruined, wretched, excessive sinner.' Nor are these the mere ink-horn terms of which our prayer-books are full, or the usual insincere devotions of which our public worship is full. It is the truth, it is the sincerity, it is the intensity, it is the absolute agony of Andrewes's supremely sinful and supremely miserable heart that so fascinates us, and holds us, and makes us like clay in his hands.

> Small is the blind man's grief to theirs who see
> Nothing at all but their own misery.

'But I have an Advocate with Thee to Thee, and may He be the propitiation for my sins Who is also the propitiation for the whole world.' As much as to say that the whole world and Lancelot Andrewes together will complete the propitiation. As much as to say that Lancelot Andrewes is a whole guilty world in himself, and that to be the propitiation for Lancelot Andrewes is more than to redeem and restore the whole world apart from him. Whom God hath set forth to be the propitiation for the whole world and Lancelot Andrewes.

His infamy.   You will sometimes see in the wall of a church

or in the wall of a house or in the wall of a garden
a stone with the smooth mark of the boring-iron
still upon it—the boring-iron by means of which
the blast was let in which shattered the hard rock
into a thousand pieces. And many such significant
marks occur all up and down the *Private Devotions*.
'I have perverted that which was right, and yet
Thou hast not overwhelmed me with infamy.' Now,
'infamy,' remarkably enough, is the very word that
an able historical writer of our day has applied to
Andrewes's share in the Essex case. Sometimes
one single sin will blast and ruin a man's whole
after-life to himself. Sometimes one single sin
will still leave its mark on a man long long after it
has been forsaken, repented of, atoned for, and forgiven. One single sin will so explode and shatter
his conscience, it will so bruise and break his heart
into a thousand pieces, that like one of the Children
of Israel a true penitent will feel the taste of the dust
of the golden calf in every cup he ever after drinks
—in his sweetest as well as in his bitterest cup. The
Essex case followed Andrewes about all his days,
as his drunkenness followed Noah, and his adultery
David, and the sins of his blasphemy and injurious-
ness Paul, and our sins us. 'God often permits sin,
even in the elect,' says Bishop Wilson, 'that He
may make their fall instrumental to their conversion
and salvation. We have reason to bless God for
those sins that awaken us, lead us to repentance,
and make us to love much because so much has
been forgiven us.' 'Wherewithal a man sinneth,'
says the Son of Sirach, 'by the same also shall he
be punished. Thou, O God, tormentest men with
their own abominations.' Or as Andrewes has it,
'Let not my ungodliness be for my punishment.

Destroy me not in mine iniquities, nor reserve evil for me, nor make me a public shame.' We stare at the length and at the number of the hours that Andrewes spent every day with sweating hands, but when God begins to torment us with our own abominations, and to make our ungodliness our punishment, all Andrewes's hours will have flown past, and we shall neither have numbered them nor grudged them.

His power over us.

'I return to my own heart, and with all my heart I return to Thee, O God of penitents, O Saviour of sinners. Evening by evening will I return in the innermost marrow of my soul. I turn back from my evil ways, I return unto mine own heart, and with my whole heart I return unto Thee, saying, I know, O Lord, the plague of my heart. Since the days of my youth have I been in a great trespass unto this day, and I cannot stand before Thee, by reason of this. I bear the brands of sin. I conceal nothing. I make no excuses. I have destroyed myself. I am without plea. Thou art just in all that has come upon me. Thou hast done right, but I have done wickedly. I remember my sins in the bitterness of my soul. I have no rest because of them. I turn away from them and groan. I despise and hate myself. Forgive me, for I knew not, truly I knew not what I did when I sinned against Thee. I can sin much, but I cannot return from my sins. Only, I will always remember my latter end. I will give myself up to prayer. I will give up the rest of my life to repentance, because Thou art waiting for my full conversion.' How his words transfix us! How our past comes back upon us at his words! How our hearts melt in us as Andrewes takes us by the hand, and as we kneel beside him! The secret of the Lord and His best power are with this penitent in a most singular way, till that wonderful book of his in every page of it pierces us, solemnises us, and subdues us to tears and to prayer and to obedience as no other book of its kind has ever done. Every page, almost every line, of the *Private Devotions* has some strong word in it, some startling word, some selected, compounded, and compacted word, some heart-laden clause, some scriptural or liturgical expression set in a blaze of new light and life, and ever after to be filled with new power as we employ it in our own prayers and praises. It is true genius; it is a gift of God and a grace of His Spirit of no common kind to be able in this way to make the old and familiar language of devotion so new, so quick, so powerful, and so prevailing, as Andrewes makes it in this fine book of his which is now open before us.

A TRANSCRIPT OF
THE DEVOTIONS

Times of Prayer.

Always.—*Our Lord.*

Without ceasing.—*Paul.*

At all seasons.—*Paul.*

He kneeled upon his knees three times a day, and prayed, and gave thanks before his God, as he did aforetime.—*Daniel.*

Evening, and morning, and at noon, will I pray, and cry aloud : and He shall hear my voice.—*David.*

Seven times a day do I praise Thee.—*David.*

1. In the morning, a great while before day.—*Our Lord.*

2. The dawning of the morning.—*David.*

3. The third hour of the day.—*Peter.*

4. About the sixth hour.—*Peter.*

5. At the hour of prayer, the ninth.—*Peter and John.*

6. At the eventide.—*Isaac.*

7. By night.—*The Servants of the Lord.*

At midnight.—*David.*

Places of Prayer.

In all places where I record My name, I will come unto thee, and I will bless thee.—*The Lord to Moses.*

That Thine eyes may be open toward this house night and day, even toward the place of which Thou hast said, My name shall be there : that Thou mayest hearken unto the prayer which Thy servant shall make toward this place.—*Solomon.*

As for me, I will come into Thy house
in the multitude of Thy mercy:
and in Thy fear will I worship
toward Thy holy temple.
Hear the voice of my supplications,
when I cry unto Thee,
when I lift up my hands
toward Thy holy oracle.
We have thought of Thy lovingkindness, O God,
in the midst of Thy temple.—*David.*

In the assembly of the upright, and in the congregation.—*David.*

Enter into thy closet, and when thou hast shut thy door, pray to thy Father Which is in secret.—*Our Lord.*

They went up into an upper room.—*The Apostles.*

He went up upon the housetop to pray.—*Peter.*

They went up together into the temple.—*Peter and John.*

We kneeled down on the shore, and prayed.—*Paul and the disciples at Tyre.*

He went forth over the brook Cedron, where was a garden, into the which He entered.—*Our Lord.*

Let them sing aloud upon their beds.—*The Saints.*

He withdrew Himself into the wilderness, and prayed.—*Our Lord.*

I will therefore that men pray everywhere, lifting up holy hands, without wrath and doubting.—*Paul.*

Circumstances and Accompaniments of Prayer.

He kneeled down and prayed.—*Our Lord.*
He went a little farther, and fell on His face, and prayed.—*Our Lord.*

Moses made haste, and bowed his head toward the earth, and worshipped.
Our soul is bowed down to the dust,
    our belly cleaveth unto the earth.—*David.*
I am ashamed and blush to lift up my face to Thee, my God.—*Ezra.*
Standing afar off, he would not lift up so much as his eyes unto heaven, but smote upon his breast. —*The Publican.*
He came trembling.—*The Philippian Jailor.*
We mourn sore like doves.—*Isaiah.*
Mine eyes are ever toward the Lord.—*David.*
I stretch forth my hands unto Thee.—*David.*
Let the lifting up of my hands be as the evening sacrifice.—*David.*
All the day long have I been plagued, and chastened every morning.—*David.*

For behold this selfsame thing, that ye sorrowed after a godly sort, what carefulness it wrought in you, yea, what clearing of yourselves, yea, what indignation, yea, what fear, yea, what vehement desire, yea, what zeal, yea, what revenge !—*Paul.*

COURSE OF MORNING PRAYERS FOR THE SEVEN DAYS OF THE WEEK.

The First Day.

1. MEDITATION AND ADORATION.

THROUGH the tender mercy of our God
the dayspring from on high hath visited us.

Glory be to Thee, O Lord, glory to Thee,
   Creator of the light, Enlightener of the world.
   God is the Lord, Who hath shewed us light:
         bind the sacrifice with cords,
         even unto the horns of the altar.
Glory be to Thee for the visible light:
         the sun's radiance, the flame of fire;
         day and night, evening and morning;
   for the light invisible and intellectual:
         that which may be known of God,
         that which is written in the law,
         oracles of prophets,
         melody of psalms,
         instruction of proverbs,
         experience of histories—
   a light which never sets.

By Thy resurrection raise us up
   unto newness of life,
         supplying to us frames of repentance.
The God of peace, that brought again from the dead
   our Lord Jesus,

that great Shepherd of the sheep,
   through the blood of the everlasting covenant,
make us perfect in every good work to do His will,
working in us that which is well pleasing in His
      sight,
   through Jesus Christ ;
   to Whom be glory for ever and ever.

Thou Who didst send down on Thy disciples
   Thy Thrice-Holy Spirit on this day,
    take not Thou the gift, O Lord, from us,
but renew it, day by day, in us, who ask Thee for it.

2. CONFESSION OF SIN.

Merciful and pitiful Lord,
   longsuffering and full of compassion,
I have sinned, Lord, I have sinned against Thee ;
   O wretched man that I am,
   I have sinned, Lord, against Thee
     much and grievously,
   in observing lying vanities.

I conceal nothing : I make no excuses.
I give Thee glory, O Lord, this day.
I denounce against myself my sins.
Indeed I have sinned against the Lord,
   and thus and thus have I done.
I have sinned and perverted that which was right,
   and it profited me not.

And what shall I now say ?
   or with what shall I open my mouth ?
What shall I answer, seeing I have done it ?
Without plea, without excuse, self-condemned am I.

I have destroyed myself.
O Lord, righteousness belongeth unto Thee,
but unto me confusion of face.
And Thou art just in all that is brought upon me
for Thou hast done right,
but I have done wickedly.
And now, Lord, what is my hope?
Art not Thou, Lord?
Truly my hope is even in Thee,
if hope of salvation remaineth to me,
if Thy lovingkindness vanquisheth
the multitude of my iniquities.

O remember what my substance is,
the work of Thy hands,
the likeness of Thy countenance,
the reward of Thy blood,
a name from Thy name,
a sheep of Thy pasture,
a son of Thy covenant.
Forsake not Thou the work of Thine own hands.
Hast Thou made in vain
Thine own image and likeness?
In vain, if thou destroy it.
And what profit is there in my blood?
Thine enemies will rejoice.
May they never rejoice, O Lord.
Grant not to them my destruction.

Look upon the face of Thine Anointed,
and in the blood of Thy covenant,
in the propitiation for the sins of the whole world.
Lord, be merciful to me a sinner,
even to me, O Lord, of sinners
the first, the chief, and the greatest.
For Thy name's sake, O Lord, pardon mine iniquity,

for it is great; greater cannot be.
For Thy name's sake, that name
beside which none other under heaven
is given among men,
whereby we must be saved,
the Spirit Himself helping our infirmities,
and making intercession for us
with groanings that cannot be uttered.
For the fatherly yearnings of the Father,
the bloody wounds of the Son,
the unutterable groanings of the Spirit,
O Lord, hear; O Lord, forgive;
O Lord, hearken and do;
defer not, for Thine own sake,
O my God.

For I acknowledge my transgressions:
and my sin is ever before me;
I remember my sins in the bitterness of my soul,
I am sorry for them;
I turn back with groans,
I have indignation and revenge
and wrath against myself.
I abhor and bruise myself
that my penitence, Lord, O Lord,
is not deeper, is not fuller;
Lord, I repent,
help Thou mine impenitence;
and more, and still more,
pierce Thou, rend, crush my heart.

And remit, pardon, forgive
all things that are grief unto me
and offence of heart.
Cleanse Thou me from secret faults,
keep back Thy servant also from presumptuous sins.

Magnify Thy mercies towards the utter sinner;
and in season, Lord, say to me,
Be of good cheer; thy sins are forgiven thee;
My grace is sufficient for thee.
Say unto my soul, I am thy salvation.
Why art thou cast down, O my soul?
and why art thou disquieted in me?
Return unto thy rest, O my soul;
for the Lord hath dealt bountifully with thee.

O Lord, rebuke me not in Thine anger,
neither chasten me in Thy hot displeasure.
I said, I will confess my transgressions unto the Lord;
and Thou forgavest the iniquity of my sin.
Lord, all my desire is before Thee;
and my groaning is not hid from Thee.
Have mercy upon me, O God,
according to Thy lovingkindness:
according unto the multitude of Thy tender mercies
blot out my transgressions.
Thou shalt arise, and have mercy on me, O Lord,
for the time to favour me, yea, the set time, is come.
If Thou, Lord, shouldest mark iniquities,
O Lord, who shall stand?
Enter not into judgment with Thy servant:
for in Thy sight shall no man living be justified.

3. PRAYER FOR GRACE.

My hands will I lift up
unto Thy commandments, which I have loved.
Open Thou mine eyes and I shall see,
incline my heart and I shall desire,
order my steps and I shall walk
in the way of Thy commandments.

O Lord God, be Thou to me a God,
and besides Thee let there be none else,
no other, nought else with Thee.

Vouchsafe to me, to worship Thee and serve Thee
according to Thy commandments:

in truth of spirit,

in reverence of body,

in blessing of lips,

both in private and in public;
to pay honour to them that have the rule over me,

by obedience and submission;
to shew affection to my own, by care and providence;
to overcome evil with good;
to possess my vessel in sanctification and honour;
to be free from the love of money,

content with such things as I have;
to speak the truth in love;
to be desirous not to lust, not to lust passionately,

not to walk after lusts.

THE HEDGE OF THE LAW.

To bruise the serpent's head.

To consider my latter end.

To cut off occasions of sin.

To be sober.

Not to sit idle.

To shun the wicked.

To cleave to the good.

To make a covenant with the eyes.

To bring the body into subjection.

To give myself unto prayer.

To come to repentance.

Hedge up my way with thorns,
that I find not the path for following vanity.

Hold Thou me in with bit and bridle,
lest I come not near to Thee.
O Lord, compel me to come in to Thee.

4. CONFESSION OF FAITH.

I believe, O Lord, in Thee,
Father, Word, Spirit, One God;
that by Thy fatherly love and power
all things were created;
that by Thy goodness and love to man
all things have been gathered together into one
in Thy Word,
Who, for us men and for our salvation,
became flesh,
was conceived, was born,
suffered, was crucified,
died, was buried,
descended, rose again,
ascended, sat down,
will return, will repay;
that by the forth-shining and operation
of Thy Holy Spirit
hath been called out of the whole world
a peculiar people, into a commonwealth
of faith in the truth
and holiness of life,
in which we are partakers
of the communion of saints
and forgiveness of sins in this world,
and in which we look for
the resurrection of the flesh
and the life everlasting
in the world to come.

This most holy faith once delivered to the saints
       I believe, O Lord;
         help Thou mine unbelief,
          increase Thou my little faith.

And vouchsafe to me
       to love the Father for His love,
       to reverence the Almighty for His power,
       to Him, as unto a faithful Creator, to commit
          my soul in well doing.
Vouchsafe to me to partake
       from Jesus of salvation,
       from Christ of anointing,
       from the only begotten Son of adoption ;
  to serve the Lord
       for His conception, in faith,
       for His birth, in humility,
       for His sufferings, in patience and in impatience
          of sin ;
       for His cross, to crucify occasions of sin,
       for His death, to mortify the flesh,
       for His burial, to bury evil thoughts in good
          works,
       for His descent, to meditate upon hell,
       for His resurrection, upon newness of life,
       for His ascension, to set my mind on things above,
       for His sitting on high, to set my mind on the
          better things on His right hand,
       for His return, to fear His second appearing,
       for His judgment, to judge myself ere I be judged.
From the Spirit
    vouchsafe to me to receive the breath of saving grace,
       in the holy Catholic Church
to have my own calling, sanctification, and portion,
       and fellowship of her holy things,

prayers, fastings, groanings,
watchings, tears, sufferings,
for assurance of the remission of sins,
for hope of resurrection and translation
to eternal life.

5. INTERCESSION.

O Thou that art the confidence of all the ends of
the earth,
and of them that are afar off upon the sea :
O Thou in Whom our fathers trusted,
and Thou didst deliver them :
in Whom they trusted,
and were not confounded :
Thou Who art my trust from my youth,
from my mother's breasts :
upon Whom I was cast from the womb,
be Thou my hope now and evermore,
and my portion in the land of the living.

In Thy nature,
in Thy names,
in Thy types,
in Thy word,
in Thy deed,
my Hope,
disappoint me not of this my hope.

O Hope of all the ends of the earth,
remember Thy whole creation for good,
visit the world in Thy compassion.
O Guardian of men, O sovereign Lord, Lover of men,
remember all our race ;
Thou Who hast concluded all in unbelief,
have mercy upon all, O Lord.

O Thou Who to this end didst die and live again,
 to be Lord both of the dead and living,
   live we or die we,
   Thou art our Lord;
  have mercy upon all, O Lord.
O Helper of the helpless,
  refuge in times of trouble,
  remember all who are in necessity
   and need Thy succour.

O God of grace and truth,
  establish all who stand in truth and grace;
 restore all who are sick with heresies and sins.
O saving Strength of Thine anointed,
   remember Thy congregation
which Thou hast purchased and redeemed of old;
   O grant to all that believe
  to be of one heart and one soul.
Thou Who walkest in the midst of the golden
   candlesticks,
 remove not our candlestick out of its place;
 set in order the things that are wanting,
 strengthen the things which remain,
  which are ready to die.

O Lord of the harvest,
 send forth labourers, made sufficient by Thee,
   into Thy harvest.
O Portion of those
   who wait in Thy temple,
   grant to our clergy
 rightly to divide the word of truth,
and to walk uprightly according thereto;
 grant to thy people who love Thee
to obey and submit themselves to them.

O King of nations unto the ends
of the earth,
strengthen all the states
of the inhabited world,
as being Thine ordinance,
though a creation of man;
scatter Thou the peoples that delight in war;
make wars to cease unto the end of the earth.
O Expectation of the isles, and their Hope,
Lord, save this island,
and all the country in which we sojourn,
from all affliction, peril, and need.

Lord of lords, Ruler of rulers, remember all rulers
to whom Thou hast given rule in the earth;
and O remember specially our divinely guarded king,
and work with him more and more,
and prosper his way in all things;
speak good things unto his heart
for Thy Church and all Thy people;
grant to him profound and perpetual peace,
that in his tranquillity
we may lead a quiet and peaceable life
in all godliness and honesty.

O Thou by Whom the powers that be are ordained,
grant to those who are chief in court
to be chief in virtue and Thy fear;
grant to the council Thy holy wisdom;
to our mighty men, to have no might against
but for the truth;
to the courts of law Thy judgments,
to judge all in all things
without preference, without partiality.
O God of hosts,
give a prosperous course and strength

to all the Christian army
against the enemies of our most holy faith.
Grant to our population
to be subject unto the higher powers,
not only because of the wrath, but also for conscience
sake.
Grant to farmers and graziers good seasons ;
to the fleet and fishers fair weather ;
to tradesmen, not to overreach one another ;
to mechanics, to pursue their business lawfully,
down to the humblest workman, down to the poor.

O God, not of us only but of our seed,
bless our children within us,
that they may grow in wisdom as in stature,
and in favour with Thee and with men.
Thou Who wouldest have us provide for our own,
and hatest those without natural affection,
remember, Lord, my kinsmen according to the flesh ;
grant me to speak peace concerning them,
and to seek their good.
Thou Who wouldest have us make return to our
benefactors,
remember, Lord, for good
all from whom I have received good ;
keep them alive and bless them upon the earth,
and deliver them not
unto the will of their enemies.
Thou Who hast noted the man who neglects his own
as worse than an infidel,
remember in Thy good pleasure
all those in my household ;
peace be to my house,
children of peace be all who dwell in it.
Thou Who wouldest that our righteousness exceed
the righteousness of sinners,

grant me, Lord, to love those who love me ;
    my own friends, and my father's friends,
and my friends' children, never to forsake.

Thou Who wouldest that we overcome evil with good,
    and pray for those who persecute us,
have pity on mine enemies, Lord, as on me ;
    and lead them together with me
    to Thy heavenly kingdom.
Thou Who grantest the prayers thy servants make
    one for another,
    remember, Lord, for good, and pity
all those who remember me in their prayers,
or whom I have promised to remember in mine.

Thou Who acceptest the willing mind in every good
    work,
    remember, Lord, as if they prayed to Thee,
    those who for any sufficient cause
    have not time for prayer.
Arise, and have mercy
    on those who are in the last necessity ;
for the time to favour them, yea, the set time, is come.
Thou shalt have mercy on them, O Lord,
    as on me also, when in extremities.

Remember, Lord,
infants, children, the growing youth, the young men,
    the middle-aged, the old, the decayed,
    hungry, thirsty, naked, sick,
    captives, friendless strangers,
    possessed with devils and tempted to suicide,
    troubled by unclean spirits,
the sick in soul or body, the fainthearted, the
    despairing,

all in prison and chains, all under sentence of death,
orphans, widows, foreigners, travellers, voyagers,
women with child, women who give suck,
all in bitter servitude, or mines, or galleys,
or in loneliness.

O Lord, Thou preservest man and beast.
How excellent is Thy lovingkindness, O God!
Therefore the children of men put their trust
under the shadow of Thy wings.

The Lord bless us, and keep us:
the Lord make His face shine upon us,
and be gracious unto us:
the Lord lift up His countenance upon us,
and give us peace.

I commend to Thee, O Lord,
my soul, and my body,
my mind, and my thoughts,
my prayers, and my vows,
my senses, and my members,
my words, and my works,
my life, and my death;
my brothers, my sisters, and their children;
my friends, my benefactors, my well-wishers,
those who have a claim on me,
my kindred, my neighbours,
my country, and all Christian people.

I commend to Thee, Lord,
my impulses, and my occasions,
my resolves, and my attempts,
my going out, and my coming in,
my sitting down, and my rising up.

6. THANKSGIVING.

How truly meet, and right, and comely, and due,
in all, and for all things,
in all times, places, manners,
in every season, every spot,
everywhere, always, altogether,
to remember Thee, to worship Thee,
to confess to Thee, to praise Thee,
to bless Thee, to hymn Thee,
to give thanks to Thee,
Maker, Nourisher, Guardian, Governor,
Healer, Benefactor, Perfecter of all,
Lord and Father, King and God,
Fountain of life and immortality,
Treasure of everlasting goods,
Whom the heavens hymn,
and the heaven of heavens,
the angels and all the heavenly powers,
one to other crying continually,—
and we the while, weak and unworthy,
under their feet,—
Holy, holy, holy, Lord God of Hosts :
full is the whole heaven, and the whole earth,
of the majesty of Thy glory.

Blessed be the glory of the Lord out of His place,
for His Godhead, His mysteriousness,
His height, His sovereignty, His almightiness,
His eternity, His providence.

The Lord is my strength, my strong rock, my defence,
my deliverer, my succour, my buckler,
the horn of my salvation, my refuge.

The Second Day.

1. MEDITATION AND ADORATION.

My voice shalt Thou hear in the morning, O Lord;
in the morning
will I direct my prayer unto Thee,
and will look up.

Blessed art Thou, O Lord,
Who didst create the firmament of heaven,
the heavens and the heaven of heavens,
the heavenly powers,
angels, archangels,
cherubim, seraphim;
the waters above the heavens,
mists and vapours,
for showers, dew, hail, snow as wool,
hoar frost as ashes, ice as morsels,
clouds from the ends of the earth;
lightnings, thunders, winds out of Thy treasuries,
storms;
the waters beneath the heavens,
water to drink,
water to wash in.

2. CONFESSION OF SIN.

I will confess my iniquity,
and the iniquity of my fathers,
for I have transgressed, and neglected Thee, O Lord,
and walked perversely before Thee.

Set not, O Lord, set not mine iniquities before Thee,
nor my secret sins in the light of Thy countenance,
but pardon the iniquity of Thy servant,
according to Thy great mercy,
as Thou hast been merciful to him from a child,
even until now.

I have sinned; what shall I do unto Thee,
O Thou preserver of men?
Why hast Thou set me as a mark against Thee,
so that I am a burden to myself?
O pardon my transgression,
and take away mine iniquity.
Deliver me from going down to the pit,
for Thou hast found a ransom.

Have mercy on me, O Lord, Thou Son of David.
Lord, help me.
Truth, Lord; yet the dogs eat of the crumbs
which fall from their masters' table.

Have patience with me, Lord;
yet I have not wherewith to pay, I confess to Thee;
forgive me the whole debt, I beseech Thee.

How long wilt Thou forget me, O Lord? for ever?
How long wilt Thou hide Thy face from me?
How long shall I take counsel in my soul,
having sorrow in my heart daily?
How long shall mine enemy be exalted over me?
Consider and hear me, O Lord my God;
lighten mine eyes, lest I sleep the sleep of death;
lest mine enemy say, I have prevailed against him;
and those that trouble me rejoice when I am moved.
But I have trusted in Thy mercy;

my heart shall rejoice in Thy salvation.
I will sing unto the Lord,
because He hath dealt bountifully with me.

3. PRAYER FOR GRACE.

Remove from me all iniquity and profanity,
    superstition and hypocrisy ;
    worship of idols and worship of men ;
    rash oath and curse ;
    neglect or indecency of worship ;
    haughtiness and recklessness ;
    strife and wrath ;
    passion and corruption ;
    indolence and fraud ;
    lying and injuriousness ;
    every evil notion, every impure thought, every
        base desire, every unseemly thought.
Grant to me
    to be godly and devout ;
    to worship and to serve ;
    to bless and to swear truly ;
    to confess becomingly in the congregation ;
    affection and obedience ;
    patience and good temper ;
    purity and temperance ;
    contentedness and goodness ;
    truth and incorruptness ;
    good thoughts, and perseverance to the end.

4. CONFESSION OF FAITH.

I believe in God
    the Father Almighty, Maker of heaven and earth
    and in Jesus Christ His only begotten Son our Lord,

Who was conceived by the Holy Ghost,
born of the Virgin Mary,
suffered under Pontius Pilate,
was crucified,
dead,
and buried :
He descended into hell ;
He rose again from the dead ;
He ascended into heaven,
and sitteth on the right hand ;
to return thence
to judge both quick and dead.
I believe in the Holy Ghost ;
in the Church,
holy,
Catholic,
the communion of saints ;
in the forgiveness of sins,
the resurrection of the flesh,
and the life everlasting.

And now, Lord, what wait I for ?
My hope is in Thee ;
in Thee, O Lord, have I trusted,
let me never be confounded.

5. INTERCESSION.

Let us pray the Lord for the whole creation :
for the supply of seasons,
healthful, fruitful, peaceful ;
for the whole race of mankind :
for those who are not Christians,
that atheists, ungodly, Pagans, Turks, Jews
may be converted ;

for all Christians :
    for restoration of all
        who languish in errors and sins ;
    for confirmation of all
        who have been granted truth and grace ;
for succour and comfort of all
    who are dispirited, infirm, distressed, unsettled
                men and women ;
for thankfulness and sobriety in all
    who are hearty, healthy, prosperous, quiet,
                men and women ;

for the Catholic Church,
        its establishment and increase ;
    for the Eastern,
        its deliverance and union ;
    for the Western,
        its adjustment and peace ;
    for the British,
        the supply of the things that are wanting in it,
        the strengthening of the things that remain
        in it ;
for the episcopate, presbytery, Christian people ;

for the states of the inhabited world ;
    for Christian states, far off, near at hand ;
    for our own ;
for all in rule ;
    for our divinely guarded king,
    for those who have place at court ;
    for council and judicature,
                army and police,
    commons and their leaders,
        farmers, graziers, fishers, merchants,
           traders, and mechanics,

down to the humblest workmen, and the poor;
for the succession :
    for the good nurture of all the royal family,
        of the young ones of the nobility;
for all in universities, in inns of court, in schools,
        at work, in town or country;

for those who have a claim on me
    from kinship,—
      for brothers and sisters,
        that God's blessing may be on them,
          and on their children;
    or from benefits conferred,—
        that Thy recompence may be on all
          who have benefited me,
     who have ministered to me in carnal things;
    or from trust placed in me,—
      for all whom I have educated,
      all whom I have ordained,
      for my college, my parish,
      Southwell, St Paul's, Westminster,
      dioceses of Chichester, Ely, and my present,
      clergy, people, helps, governments,
      the deanery of the chapel royal,
      the almonry,
      the colleges committed to me;
    or from natural kindness,—
      for all who love me,
        though I know them not;
    or from Christian love,—
      for those who hate me without cause,
some, too, even on account of truth and righteous-
              ness;
    or from neighbourhood,—
      for all who dwell near me

peaceably and harmlessly ;
or from promise,—
 for all whom I have promised to remember
     in my prayers ;
or from mutual offices,—
 for all who remember me in their prayers,
    and ask of me the same ;
or from stress of engagements,—
 for all who for any sufficient cause fail to call
     upon Thee ;

for all who have no intercessor
    in their own behalf ;
for all who at present are in agony
   of extreme necessity or deep affliction ;
for all who are attempting any good work
 which will bring glory to the name of God,
   or some great good to the Church ;
for all who act nobly
 either towards things sacred or towards the poor ;
for all who have ever been offended by me
   either in word or in deed.

God be merciful unto me, and bless me ;
God make His face to shine upon me,
  and have mercy on me.
God bless me, even our God ;
God bless me, and receive my prayer.

O direct my life towards Thy commandments,
hallow my soul, purify my body, correct my thoughts,
cleanse my desires, soul and body, mind and spirit,
   heart and reins.
Renew me thoroughly, O Lord,
 for, if Thou wilt, Thou canst.

6. THANKSGIVING.

The Lord, the Lord God, merciful and gracious,
longsuffering, and abundant in goodness and truth,
keeping mercy for thousands,
forgiving iniquity and transgression and sin;
and that will by no means clear the guilty;
visiting the iniquity of the fathers upon the children.

I will bless the Lord at all times:
His praise shall continually be in my mouth.

Glory to God in the highest,
and on earth peace,
goodwill toward men.

The angels,	guardianship;
archangels,	illumination;
powers,	wonders;
thrones,	judgment;
dominions,	beneficence;
principalities,	government;
authorities,	against devils;
cherubim,	knowledge;
seraphim,	love.

In all the thoughts of our hearts,
words of our lips,
deeds of our hands,
paths of our feet.

The Third Day.

1. MEDITATION AND ADORATION.

O God, Thou art my God,
early will I seek Thee.

Blessed art Thou, O Lord,
who gatheredst the water into the sea,
and broughtest to sight the earth,
and madest to sprout herbs and fruit trees.
There are the depths and the sea as an heap,
lakes, rivers, springs ;
earth, continent, and isles,
mountains, hills, and valleys ;
glebe lands, meadows, glades,
green pasture, corn, hay ;
herbs and flowers
for food, pleasure, medicine ;
fruit trees bearing fruits,
wine, oil, and spices,
and trees for timber ;
things under the earth,
stones, metals, minerals, coals ;
blood, and fire, and vapour of smoke.

2. CONFESSION OF SIN.

Who can understand his errors ?
Cleanse Thou me from secret faults.
Keep back Thy servant also from presumptuous sins,
let them not have dominion over me.

For Thy name's sake, O Lord,
pardon mine iniquity, for it is great.

My iniquities have taken hold upon me,
so that I am not able to look up ;'
they are more than the hairs of my head
therefore my heart faileth me.
Be pleased, O Lord, to deliver me ;
O Lord, make haste to help me.
Shew thy marvellous lovingkindness,
O Thou that savest them that trust in Thee.
I said, Lord, have mercy upon me,
heal my soul, for I have sinned against Thee.

I have sinned, but I am confounded,
and I turn back from my evil ways;
I return unto mine own heart,
and with my whole heart I return unto Thee ;
and I seek Thy face, and I beseech Thee, saying,
I have sinned, I have committed iniquity,
I have done unjustly.
I know, O Lord, the plague of my heart,
and lo, I return to Thee with all my heart,
and with all my strength.

And Thou, O Lord, now from Thy dwelling place,
and from the glorious throne of Thy kingdom
in heaven,
hear the prayer and the supplication of Thy servant :
and be merciful to Thy servant, and heal his soul.

God be merciful to me a sinner,
be merciful to me the chief of sinners.
Father, I have sinned against heaven, and before Thee,
and am no more worthy to be called Thy son,

> make me one of Thy hired servants;
> make me one, even if the last,
> or the least among all.

3. PRAYER FOR GRACE.

> What profit is there in my blood,
> when I go down to the pit?
> shall the dust praise Thee? shall it declare Thy truth?
> Hear, O Lord, and have mercy upon me;
> Lord, be Thou my Helper;
> turn my mourning into dancing,
> my dreamings into earnestness,
> my falls into clearings of myself,
> my guilt into indignation, my sin into fear,
> my transgression into vehement desire,
> my unrighteousness into zeal,
> my pollution into revenge.

4. CONFESSION OF FAITH.

> Godhead: love, power,
>   providence.
> Salvation: anointing, adoption,
>   dominion;
>   conception, birth, sufferings,
>   cross, death, burial;
>   descent, resurrection, ascension,
>   sitting, return, judgment.
> Breath: holiness,
>   calling, hallowing,
>   communion of saints and of saintly things,
>   forgiveness of sins,
>   resurrection,
>   life eternal.

5. INTERCESSION.

For all creatures :
  men,
  persons compassed
    with infirmity ;
for Churches :
  Catholic,
  Eastern,
  Western,
  our own ;
for the episcopate,
  presbytery,
  clergy,
  Christian people ;
for the states
  of the whole earth,
  Christian,
  neighbouring,
  our own ;
for rulers :
  kings,
  Godfearing,
  our own ;
for councillors,
  judges,
  nobles,
  men of war,
    on land,
    on sea ;

for the people :
  the succession,
  schools,
  those at court,
    in cities,
    in the country ;
for those who minister
  to the soul,
  to the body,
  food,
  raiment,
  health,
  things that pertain
    to this life ;
for those who have
  a claim on me :
    by birth,
    through benefits,
    from trust
      now or formerly,
    through friendship,
    love,
    neighbourhood,
  from promise,
    mutual offices,
    want of leisure,
    destitution,
    extremity.

6. THANKSGIVING.

We praise Thee, O God,
for Thy goodness, grace, love,
kindness, and love toward men;
for Thy meekness and gentleness,
Thy forbearance and longsuffering;
for Thine abundant mercy,
Thy mercies, the multitude of Thy tender mercies,
bowels of mercies.

The Lord is pitiful,
very pitiful, and of tender mercy.
He passeth by the transgression of the remnant of
His heritage.
The times of ignorance God overlooked.
Have not I held My peace even of long time?
Many times didst Thou deliver them.
Many years didst Thou bear with them.
He doth not afflict willingly.
He did not stir up all His wrath.
He hath not rewarded us according to our iniquities.
He retaineth not His anger for ever.
In wrath He remembereth mercy.
Speak ye comfortably to Jerusalem, and cry unto her,
that her warfare is accomplished,
that her iniquity is pardoned:
for she hath received of the Lord's hand
double for all her sins.
The Lord is ready to forgive,
to be reconciled,
to be propitiated.

The Fourth Day.

1. MEDITATION AND ADORATION.

I HAVE meditated on Thee, O Lord,
in the night watches,
for Thou hast been my help.

Blessed art Thou, O Lord,
Who madest the two lights, sun and moon,
greater and lesser,
and the stars also,
for light, for signs, and for seasons,
for spring, summer, autumn, winter,
for days, and weeks, and months, and years,
to rule over day and night.

2. CONFESSION OF SIN.

Behold, Thou art wroth; for we have sinned.
We are all as an unclean thing,
and all our righteousnesses are as filthy rags;
and we all do fade as a leaf;
and our iniquities, like the wind,
have taken us away.
But now, O Lord, Thou art our Father;
we are the clay, and Thou our potter,
and we all are the work of Thy hand.
Be not wroth very sore, O Lord,
neither remember iniquity for ever:

behold, see, we beseech Thee,
we are all Thy people.

O Lord, though our iniquities testify against us,
do Thou it for Thy name's sake:
for our backslidings are many;
we have sinned against thee.
Yet Thou, O Lord, art in the midst of us,
and we are called by Thy name;
leave us not.
O the Hope of Israel,
the Saviour thereof in time of trouble,
why shouldest Thou be as a stranger in the land,
and as a wayfaring man that turneth aside
to tarry for a night?
why shouldest Thou be as a man astonied,
as a mighty man that cannot save?
Be merciful to our unrighteousness,
and our sins and iniquities remember no more.

Lord, I am carnal, sold under sin;
there dwelleth in me, that is, in my flesh,
no good thing;
for the good that I would, I do not:
but the evil which I would not, that I do.
I consent unto the law that it is good,
I delight in it after the inward man;
but I see another law in my members,
warring against the law of my mind,
and bringing me into captivity to the law of sin.
O wretched man that I am,
who shall deliver me from the body of this death?
I thank God through Jesus Christ,
that where sin abounded grace did much more abound.
O Lord, Thy goodness leadeth me to repentance:

O give me, I beseech Thee, repentance
to recover me out of the snare of the devil,
who am taken captive by him at his will.

Sufficient for me the time past of my life
to have wrought the will of lusts,
walking in lasciviousness, revellings, drunkenness,
and in other excess of riot.
O Lamb without blemish and without spot,
Who hast redeemed me with Thy precious blood,
in that very blood pity me and save me:
in that blood, and in that very name,
besides which is none other under heaven
given among men,
whereby we must be saved.

O God, Thou knowest my foolishness;
and my sins are not hid from Thee.
Lord, all my desire is before Thee;
and my groaning is not hid from Thee.
Let not them that wait on Thee,
O Lord God of hosts,
be ashamed for my sake:
let not those that seek Thee be confounded
for my sake,
O God of Israel.
Deliver me out of the mire, and let me not sink:
let me be delivered from them that hate me,
and out of the deep waters.
Let not the waterflood drown me,
neither let the deep swallow me up,
and let not the pit shut her mouth upon me.

3. PRAYER FOR GRACE.

Defend me from

pride	Amorite.
envy	Hittite.
wrath	Perizzite.
gluttony	Girgashite.
lasciviousness	Hivite.
covetousness	Canaanite.
sloth	Jebusite.

Give me
humility, pitifulness, patience,
sobriety, purity, contentment, ready zeal.

One thing have I desired of the Lord,
that will I seek after;
that I may dwell in the house of the Lord
all the days of my life,
to behold the beauty of the Lord,
and to enquire in His temple.
Two things have I required of Thee, O Lord;
deny me them not before I die:
remove far from me vanity and lies:
give me neither poverty nor riches;
feed me with food convenient for me:
lest I be full, and deny Thee,
and say, Who is the Lord?
or lest I be poor and steal,
and take the name of my God in vain.
Let me learn to abound, let me learn to suffer need,
in whatsoever state I am, therewith to be content;
for nothing earthly, temporal, corruptible,
let me ever long or wait.

Grant me a happy life
in all godliness and gravity,
in all purity and nobleness,
in cheerfulness, in health, in good report,
in contentment, in safety, in freedom, in tranquillity;
a happy death, a deathless happiness.

4. CONFESSION OF FAITH.

I believe in the Father's lovingkindness;
in the Almighty's saving power;
in the Creator's providence
for guarding, ruling, perfecting the universe;
in Jesus, for salvation;
in Christ, for the anointing of His Holy Spirit;
in the only begotten Son, for adoption;
in the Lord, for His care as our Master;
in His conception and birth,
for the cleansing of our unclean conception and birth;
in His sufferings
endured that we, whose due they were,
might not suffer;
in His cross, for the curse of the law removed;
in His death, for the sting of death taken away;
in His burial, for endless corruption in the tomb
ended;
in His descent, whither we ought,
that we might not go;
in His resurrection,
as the first fruits of them that sleep;
in His ascension, to prepare a place for us;
in His sitting, to appear and intercede for us;
in His return, to take unto Him His own;
in His judgment, to render to every man
according to his deeds;

in the Holy Ghost, for power from on high,
              transforming unto sanctity
              from without and invisibly,
              yet effectually and evidently;
in the Church, a body mystical
              of those called out of the whole world
              into a commonwealth of faith and holiness;
in the communion of saints, members of this body,
a partaking with one another of holy things,
              for assurance of the remission of sins,
              for hope of resurrection and translation
              to life everlasting.

5. INTERCESSION.

We beseech Thee,
remember all, Lord, for good;
              have pity upon all, O Sovereign Lord,
              be reconciled with us all.
Give peace to the multitudes of Thy people;
              scatter offences; abolish wars;
              stop the uprisings of heresies.
              Thy peace and love
              vouchsafe to us, O God our Saviour,
Who art the confidence of all the ends of the earth.

Remember to crown the year with Thy goodness;
              for the eyes of all wait upon Thee,
and Thou givest them their meat in due season.
              Thou openest Thine hand,
and satisfiest the desire of every living thing.

Remember Thy holy Church,
              from one end of the earth to the other;
              and give her peace,

whom Thou hast redeemed with Thy precious blood;
and establish her unto the end of the world.

Remember those who bear fruit, and act nobly,
            in Thy holy Churches,
    and who remember the poor and needy;
reward them with Thy rich and heavenly gifts;
vouchsafe to them, for things earthly, heavenly,
        for corruptible, incorruptible,
            for temporal, eternal.

Remember those who are in virginity,
            and purity, and ascetic life;
    also those who live in honourable marriage,
        in Thy reverence and Thy fear.

Remember every Christian soul
            in affliction, distress, and trial,
    and in need of Thy pity and succour;
also our brethren in captivity, prison, chains,
            and bitter bondage;
        supplying return to the wandering,
            health to the sick,
        deliverance to the captives.

Remember Godfearing and faithful kings,
    whom Thou hast accounted worthy to bear rule
            upon the earth;
especially remember, Lord, our divinely guarded king;
        strengthen his dominion,
    subdue under him all adversaries;
        speak good things to his heart
    for Thy Church and all Thy people;
vouchsafe to him deep and undisturbed peace,
        that in his serenity

we may lead a quiet and peaceable life
in all godliness and honesty.
Remember, Lord, all in power and authority,
and our brethren at court,
those who are chief in council and judgment,
and all by land and sea waging Thy wars for us.

Moreover, Lord, remember graciously
our holy fathers,
the honourable presbytery, and all the clergy,
rightly dividing the word of truth,
and walking uprightly according thereto.
Remember, Lord, our brethren around us,
praying with us in this holy hour,
for their zeal and earnestness' sake.
Remember also those who for sufficient cause are away,
and pity them and us
according to the multitude of Thy mercy.

Fill our garners with all manner of store,
preserve our marriages in peace and concord,
nourish our infants, lead forward our youth,
sustain our aged,
comfort the fainthearted,
gather together the dispersed,
restore the wanderers, and knit them to Thy holy
Catholic and Apostolic Church.

Set free the troubled with unclean spirits,
voyage with the voyagers,
travel with the travellers,
stand forth for the widow,
shield the orphan,
rescue the captive,
heal the sick.

Those who are on trial, in mines, in exile, in galleys,
in whatever affliction, necessity, and emergency,
remember, O God;
and all who need Thy great compassion;
and those who love us, and those who hate;
and those who have desired us unworthy
to make mention of them in our prayers.

All Thy people remember, O Lord, our God,
and upon all pour out Thy rich pity,
to all fulfilling their requests for salvation.
Those of whom we have not made mention,
through ignorance, forgetfulness, or number
of names,
do Thou Thyself remember, O God,
who knowest the stature and the name of each,
who knowest every one from his mother's womb.
For Thou, O Lord, art the Helper of the helpless,
the Hope of the hopeless,
the Saviour of the tempest-tossed.
the Haven of the voyager,
the Physician of the sick;
do Thou Thyself become all things to all men,
Thou Who knowest each man and his petition,
each house, and its need.

Deliver, O Lord, this city,
and all the country in which we sojourn,
from plague, famine, earthquake, flood,
fire, sword, hostile invasion, and civil war.

End the schisms of the Churches,
quell the ragings of the nations,
and receive us all into Thy kingdom,
acknowledging us as sons of light;

and Thy peace and love
vouchsafe to us, O Lord, our God.

Remember, O Lord, our God, all spirits and all flesh
which we have remembered, and which we have not.

And the close of our life,
Lord, Lord, direct in peace
to be Christian, acceptable,
and, should it please Thee, painless,
gathering us together under the feet of Thy chosen,
when Thou wilt and as Thou wilt,
only without shame and sin.

The beauty of the Lord our God be upon us :
establish Thou the work of our hands upon us ;
yea, the work of our hands establish thou it.

Be, Lord,
within me to strengthen me,
without me to guard me,
over me to shelter me,
beneath me to stablish me,
before me to guide me,
after me to forward me,
round about me to secure me.

6. THANKSGIVING.

Blessed be Thou, Lord God of Israel
our Father,
for ever and ever.
Thine, O Lord, is the greatness, and the power,
and the glory, and the victory,
and the majesty :

for all that is in the heaven and in the earth
is Thine.

The nations tremble at Thy presence,
every king and every nation.

Thine is the kingdom, O Lord,
and Thou art exalted as head above all.
Both riches and honour come of Thee,
and Thou reignest over all;
and in Thine hand is power and might;
and in Thine hand it is to make great,
and to give strength unto all.
Now therefore, our God, we thank Thee
and praise Thy glorious name.

The Fifth Day.

1. MEDITATION AND ADORATION.

SATISFY us early with Thy mercy, O Lord.

Blessed art Thou, O Lord,
who broughtest forth from the waters
the moving creature that hath life,
and whales, and winged fowl,
and didst bless them, saying,
Be fruitful and multiply.

Be Thou exalted, O God, above the heavens:
and Thy glory above all the earth.

By Thy ascension, O Lord,
draw us too after Thee,
that we set our affection on things above,
not on things on the earth.

By the marvellous mystery
of Thy holy body and precious blood,
on the evening of this day,
Lord, have mercy upon us.

2. CONFESSION OF SIN.

Thou who saidst,
‘ As I live, saith the Lord God,
I have no pleasure in the death of the wicked ;

but that the wicked turn from his way and live:
  turn ye, turn ye from your evil ways;
  for why will ye die, O house of Israel?'
    turn Thou us unto Thee, O Lord,
      and we shall be turned.
  Turn us from all our transgressions;
    so iniquity shall not be our ruin.

I have sinned, I have committed iniquity,
  I have done wickedly, even by departing
    from Thy precepts, and Thy judgments.
  O Lord, righteousness belongeth unto Thee,
  and unto me confusion of face, as at this day,
      because of my trespass
    that I have trespassed against Thee.
    Lord, to us belongeth confusion of face,
  to our kings, to our princes, and to our fathers,
      because we have sinned against Thee.
Lord, according to all Thy righteousness,
        I beseech Thee,
  let Thine anger and Thy fury be turned away,
  and cause Thy face to shine upon Thy servant.
  O my God, incline Thine ear, and hear:
  open Thine eyes and behold my desolation.
    O Lord, hear; O Lord, forgive;
      O Lord, hearken and do;
  defer not, for Thine own sake, O my God:
    for Thy servant is called by Thy name.

    In many things we offend all;
  Lord, let Thy mercy rejoice against Thy judgment
        in my sins.

If I say that I have no sin, I deceive myself,
        and the truth is not in me;

but I confess my sins many and grievous,
and Thou, O Lord, art faithful and just
to forgive me my sins when I confess them.
Yea, for this too
I have an Advocate with Thee to Thee,
Thine only begotten Son, the Righteous.
May He be the propitiation for my sins,
Who is also for the whole world.

Will the Lord cast off for ever?
and will He be favourable no more?
Is His mercy clean gone for ever?
doth His promise fail for evermore?
Hath God forgotten to be gracious?
Hath He in anger shut up His
tender mercies?
And I said, This is my infirmity:
but I will remember the years of the right hand
of the Most High.

3. PRAYER FOR GRACE.

Give grace and strength to lay aside
every weight,
and the sin which doth so easily beset us;
all filthiness
and superfluity of naughtiness,
the lust of the flesh, and the lust of the eyes,
and the pride of life,
every motion of flesh and spirit
alienated from the will of Thy holiness:
to be poor in spirit,
that I have a portion in the kingdom of heaven;
to mourn, that I be comforted;
to be meek, that I inherit the earth;

to hunger and thirst after righteousness,
that I be filled;
to be merciful, that I obtain mercy;
to be pure in heart, that I see God;
to be a peacemaker, that I be called the son of God;
to be prepared for persecutions and revilings
for righteousness' sake,
that my reward be in heaven.

4. CONFESSION OF FAITH.

I, coming to God,
believe that He is,
and that He is a rewarder of them
that diligently seek Him.
I know that my Redeemer liveth,
that He is the Christ, the Son of the living God,
that He is indeed the Saviour of the world,
that He came into the world to save sinners,
of whom I am chief.
We believe that through the grace of Jesus Christ
we shall be saved even as our fathers.

I believe to see the goodness of the Lord
in the land of the living.

Our heart shall rejoice in Him,
because we have trusted in His holy name,
in the name of the Father,
of the Saviour, Mediator,
Intercessor, Redeemer,
of the twofold Comforter,
the Lamb and the Dove.
Let Thy mercy, O Lord, be upon us,
according as we hope in Thee.

5. INTERCESSION.

Let us beseech the Lord in peace
for the heavenly peace,
and the salvation of our souls;
for the peace of the whole world;
for the stability of God's holy Churches,
and the union of them all;
for this holy house,
and those who enter it with faith and reverence;
for our holy fathers,
the honourable presbytery, the diaconate in Christ,
and all, both clergy and people;
for this holy retreat, and all the city and country,
and all the faithful who dwell therein;
for salubrious weather, fruitfulness of the earth,
and peaceful times;
for voyagers, travellers,
those who are in sickness, toil, and captivity,
and for their salvation.
Aid, save, pity, and preserve them,
O God, in Thy grace.
Let us commend ourselves, and each other,
and all our life,
to Christ our God.
To Thee, O Lord, for it is fitting,
be glory, honour, and worship.

The grace of the Lord Jesus Christ,
and the love of God,
and the communion of the Holy Ghost,
be with us all.   Amen.

I commend me and mine, and all that belongs to me,
to Him that is able to keep me from falling,
and to present me faultless
before the presence of His glory with exceeding joy,
to the only wise God our Saviour,
to Whom be glory and majesty, dominion and power,
both now and ever.
Amen.

6. THANKSGIVING.

O Lord, my Lord,
for my being, life, reason,
for nurture, protection, guidance,
for education, civil rights, religion,
for Thy gifts of grace, nature, worldly good,
for redemption, regeneration, instruction,
for my call, recall, yea, many calls besides ;
for Thy forbearance, longsuffering,
long longsuffering toward me,
many seasons, many years,
even until now ;
for all good things received, successes granted me,
good deeds done ;
for the use of things present,
for Thy promise, and my hope
of the enjoyment of good things to come ;
for my parents honest and good,
teachers kind,
benefactors never to be forgotten,
fellow-ministers who are of one mind,
hearers thoughtful,
friends sincere,
domestics faithful ;
for all who have advantaged me

by writings, sermons, conversations,
prayers, examples, rebukes, injuries;
for all these, and all others
which I know, which I know not,
open, hidden,
remembered, forgotten,
done when I wished, when I wished not,
I confess to Thee and will confess,
I bless Thee and will bless,
I give thanks to Thee and will give thanks,
all the days of my life.
Who am I, or what is my father's house,
that Thou shouldest look upon such a dead dog
as I am?
What shall I render unto the Lord
for all His benefits toward me?
for all things in which He hath spared
and borne with me until now?

Holy, holy, holy,
Thou art worthy,
O Lord and our God, the Holy One,
to receive glory, honour, and power:
for Thou hast created all things,
and for Thy pleasure they are
and were created.

The Sixth Day.

1. MEDITATION AND ADORATION.

In the morning shall my prayer prevent Thee.

Blessed art Thou, O Lord,
Who broughtest forth the beasts of the earth, and
cattle,
and every thing that creepeth upon the earth,
for food, clothing, help ;
and madest man after Thine image, to rule the earth,
and blessedst him.

The forecounsel, fashioning hand,
breath of life, image of God,
appointment over Thy works,
charge to the angels concerning him,
paradise.
Heart, reins, eyes, ears, tongue, hands, feet ;
life, sense, reason, spirit, free will,
memory, conscience ;
the revelation of God, writings of the law,
oracles of prophets, melody of psalms,
instruction of proverbs, experience of histories,
service of sacrifices.

Blessed art Thou, O Lord,
for Thy great and precious promise on this day,
concerning the life-giving seed,
and for its fulfilment in the fulness of the time
on this day.

Blessed art Thou, O Lord, for the holy passion
of this day.
O by Thy sufferings for our salvation
on this day,
save us, O Lord.

2. CONFESSION OF SIN.

I have withstood Thee, Lord,
but I return unto Thee;
I have fallen by mine iniquity,
but I take with me words,
and return unto Thee and say,
Take away all iniquity, and receive me graciously:
so will I render the fruit of my lips.

Spare us, Lord, spare,
and give not Thine heritage to reproach,
to Thine enemies.

O Lord God, forgive, I beseech Thee:
by whom shall Jacob arise? for he is small.
Repent, O Lord, for this, and it shall not be.

While observing lying vanities
I forsook my own mercy,
and am cast out of Thy sight.
When my soul fainted within me,
I remembered the Lord:
yet I will look again toward Thy holy temple;
yet hast Thou brought up my life from corruption.

Who is a God like unto Thee,
that pardoneth iniquity,

and passeth by the transgression of the remnant
of His heritage?
Thou retainest not Thine anger for ever,
because Thou delightest in mercy.
Turn again and have compassion upon us, O Lord;
subdue our iniquities;
and cast all our sins into the depths of the sea,
according to Thy truth, and according to Thy mercy.

O Lord, I have heard Thy speech and was afraid:
in wrath remember mercy.

Behold me, Lord, clothed in filthy garments;
behold Satan standing at my right hand;
yet, O Lord, by the blood of Thy covenant,
by the fountain opened for sin and for uncleanness,
take away my iniquity, and cleanse me from my sin
Save me as a brand plucked out of the fire.

Father, forgive me, for I knew not,
truly I knew not, what I did
in sinning against Thee.

Lord, remember me
when Thou comest into Thy kingdom.

Lord, lay not mine enemies' sins to their charge;
Lord, lay not my own to mine.

By Thy sweat bloody and clotted, Thy soul in agony,
Thy head crowned with thorns, bruised with staves,
Thine eyes a fountain of tears,
Thine ears full of insults,
Thy mouth moistened with vinegar and gall,

Thy face stained with spitting,
Thy neck bowed down with the burden of the cross,
Thy back ploughed with the wheals and wounds
of the scourge,
Thy pierced hands and feet,
Thy strong cry, Eli, Eli,
Thy heart pierced with the spear,
the water and blood thence flowing,
Thy body broken, Thy blood poured out,
Lord, forgive the iniquity of Thy servant,
and cover all his sin.

Turn away all Thy wrath:
turn Thyself from the fierceness of Thine anger.
Turn us, O God of our salvation,
and cause Thine anger toward us to cease.
Wilt Thou be angry with us for ever,
wilt Thou draw out Thine anger to all generations?
Wilt Thou not revive us again:
that Thy people may rejoice in Thee?
Show us Thy mercy, O Lord,
and grant us Thy salvation.

3. PRAYER FOR GRACE.

The works of the flesh:
adultery, fornication, uncleanness, lasciviousness,
idolatry, witchcraft, hatred, variance, emulations,
wrath, strife, seditions, heresies, envyings, murders,
drunkenness, revellings, and such like.

The fruit of the Spirit:
love, joy, peace,
longsuffering, gentleness, goodness,
faith, meekness, temperance.

The Spirit of wisdom and understanding,
of counsel and might,
of knowledge and of the fear of the Lord.

The gifts of the Spirit:
the word of wisdom, the word of knowledge,
faith, gifts of healing, working of miracles,
prophecy, discerning of spirits,
divers kinds of tongues, interpretation of tongues.

May Thy strong hand, O Lord, be ever my defence;
Thy mercy in Christ my salvation;
Thy word of truth my instructor;
the grace of Thy life-giving Spirit
my consolation, all along, and at last.

The soul of Christ hallow me,
and the body strengthen me,
and the blood ransom me,
and the water wash me,
and the bruises heal me,
and the sweat refresh me,
and the wound hide me.

The peace of God,
which passeth all understanding,
keep my heart and mind
in the knowledge and the love of God.

4. CONFESSION OF FAITH.

I believe that Thou hast created me:
despise not the work of Thine own hands;
that Thou madest me after Thine image and likeness:
suffer not Thy likeness to be blotted out;

that Thou hast redeemed me in Thy blood :
suffer not the reward of that redemption to perish ;
that Thou hast called me Christian after Thy name :
     disdain not Thine own title ;
that Thou hast hallowed me in regeneration :
     destroy not Thy holy work ;
that Thou hast grafted me into the good olive tree,
     the member of a mystical body :
the member of Thy mystical body cut not off.

Remember the word unto Thy servant,
upon which Thou hast caused me to hope.
My soul fainteth for Thy salvation :
     but I hope in Thy word.

5. INTERCESSION.

For the welfare and prosperity
     of the whole Christian army,
    against the enemies of our most holy faith.
For our fathers in holy things,
     and all our brotherhood in Christ.
For those who hate and those who love us.
For those who pity and those who minister to us.
For those whom we have promised
     to remember in prayer.
For the liberation of captives.
For our fathers and brethren absent.
For those who voyage by sea.
For those who lie in sickness.
Let us pray also for fruitfulness of the earth ;
     and for every soul of orthodox Christians.
Let us bless Godfearing kings,
  orthodox prelates,
     the founders of this holy retreat,

our parents,
and all our forefathers
and our brethren departed.

6. THANKSGIVING.

Thou Who, on man's transgressing Thy command,
and falling,
didst not pass him by, nor leave him, God of goodness,
but didst visit him in ways manifold,
as a tender Father,
supplying him with Thy great and precious promise
concerning the life-giving seed,
opening to him the door of faith
and of repentance unto life,
and in the fulness of the time
sending Thy Christ Himself
to take on Him the seed of Abraham,
and in the oblation of His life
to fulfil the law's obedience,
and in the sacrifice of His death
to take off the law's curse,
and in His death
to redeem the world,
and in His resurrection
to quicken it:
Thou, Who doest all things
whereby to bring again our race to Thee,
that it may be partaker
of Thy divine nature and eternal glory:
Who hast borne witness
to the truth of Thy gospel
by many and manifold wonders,
in the ever memorable converse of Thy saints,
in their supernatural endurance of torments

in the marvellous conversion of the whole world
to the obedience of faith,
without might, persuasion, compulsion :
blessed, and praised, and celebrated,
and magnified, and exalted,
and glorified, and hallowed
be Thy name,
its record, and its memory,
and every memorial of it,
both now and for evermore.

Thou art worthy to take the book,
and to open the seals thereof:
for Thou wast slain, and hast redeemed us to God
by Thy blood
out of every kindred, and tongue,
and people, and nation.

Worthy is the Lamb that was slain
to receive power, and riches, and wisdom,
and strength, and honour, and glory, and blessing.

Blessing, and honour, and glory, and power,
be unto Him that sitteth upon the throne,
and unto the Lamb,
for ever and ever.   Amen.

Salvation to our God which sitteth upon the throne,
and unto the Lamb.

Amen : Blessing, and glory, and wisdom,
and thanksgiving, and honour,
and power, and might,
be unto our God
for ever and ever.
Amen.

The Seventh Day.

1. MEDITATION AND ADORATION.

O LORD, be gracious unto us;
we have waited for Thee:
be Thou our arm every morning,
our salvation also in the time of trouble.

Blessed art Thou, O Lord,
who restedst on the seventh day
from all Thy work,
and blessedst and sanctifiedst it.

2. CONFESSION OF SIN.

O my God, I am ashamed, and blush
to lift up my face to Thee,
for mine iniquities are increased
over my head,
and my trespass is grown up unto the heavens;
since the days of my youth
have I been in a great trespass unto this day;
I cannot stand before Thee because of this.

My sins are more in number than the sand of the sea,
my iniquities are multiplied,
and I not worthy to look up
and see the height of heaven,
from the number of my unrighteousnesses;

and I have no relief,
because I have provoked Thine anger,
and done evil in Thy sight,
not doing Thy will,
not keeping Thy commandments.
And now my heart kneels to Thee,
beseeching Thy goodness.
I have sinned, O Lord, I have sinned,
and I know mine iniquities;
but I ask and beseech,
remit to me, O Lord, remit to me,
and destroy me not in mine iniquities
nor be Thou angry for ever,
nor reserve evil for me,
nor condemn me in the lowest parts of the earth.
Because Thou art God, the God of penitents,
and Thou shalt shew in me all Thy lovingkindness;
for Thou shalt save me unworthy,
according to Thy much pity,
and I will praise Thee alway.

Lord, if Thou wilt, Thou canst make me clean.
Lord, speak the word only, and I shall be healed.
Lord, save; carest Thou not that we perish?
Say to me, Be of good cheer; thy sins are forgiven
thee.
Jesus, Master, have mercy on me.
Jesus, Thou Son of David, have mercy on me;
Thou Son of David, have mercy on me.
Lord, say to me, Ephphatha.
Lord, I have no man to put me into the pool.
Lord, say to me, Thou art loosed from thine
infirmity.
Say unto my soul, I am thy salvation.
Say unto me, My grace is sufficient for thee.

How long, Lord ? wilt Thou be angry for ever ?
shall Thy jealousy burn like fire ?
O remember not against us former iniquities :
let Thy tender mercies speedily prevent us :
for we are brought very low.
Help us, O God of our salvation,
for the glory of Thy name :
and deliver us,
and purge away our sins,
For Thy name's sake.

3. PRAYER FOR GRACE.

All my failings, shortcomings, falls,
offences, trespasses, scandals,
transgressions, debts, sins,
faults, ignorances, iniquities,
impieties, unrighteousnesses, pollutions.

The guilt

be gracious unto,	pardon,
remit,	forgive,
be merciful unto,	pass by,
impute not,	charge not, remember not ;

the stain

pass by,	pass over,
hide thy face from,	overlook,
cover,	wash away,
blot out,	cleanse ;

the hurt

remit,	heal,	save from,
take off,	remove,	away with,
abolish,	annul,	disperse, annihilate ;

that they be not found, that they exist not.

Grant that, giving all diligence, I may add

to my faith	virtue ;
to virtue	knowledge ;
to knowledge	temperance ;
to temperance	patience ;
to patience	godliness ;
to godliness	brotherly kindness ;
to brotherly kindness	charity ;

and that, forgetting not the cleansing from my old
sins,
I may give diligence to make my calling
and election sure
through good works.

4. CONFESSION OF FAITH.

I believe in Thee the Father ;
behold then, if Thou art a Father and we are children,
as a father pitieth his children,
be Thou of tender mercy towards us, O Lord.
I believe in Thee, the Lord ;
behold then, if Thou art Lord and we are servants,
our eyes wait upon Thee our Lord,
until Thou have mercy upon us.
I believe that though we are neither sons nor servants,
but dogs only,
yet we have leave to eat of the crumbs
That fall from Thy table.
I believe that Christ is the Lamb of God ;
O Lamb of God, Which takest away the sin
of the world,
take Thou away mine.
I believe that Christ Jesus came into the world
to save sinners ;
Thou Who camest to save sinners,

save Thou me, of sinners
chiefest and greatest.
I believe that Christ came to save that which was
lost;
Thou Who camest to save the lost,
never suffer, O Lord, that to be lost which
Thou hast saved.
I believe that the Spirit is the Lord and Giver of
life;
Thou Who gavest me a living soul,
grant me that I receive not my soul in vain.
I believe that the Spirit gives grace
in His holy things;
grant me that I receive not His grace in vain,
nor hope of His holy things.
I believe that the Spirit maketh intercession for us
with groanings that cannot be uttered;
grant me of His intercession and those groanings
to partake, O Lord.

5. INTERCESSION.

Our fathers trusted in Thee:
they trusted, and Thou didst deliver them.
They cried unto Thee, and were delivered:
they trusted in Thee, and were not confounded.
As Thou didst our fathers in the generations of old,
so also deliver us, O Lord,
who trust in Thee.

O Heavenly King,
confirm our faithful kings,
stablish the faith,
soften the nations,
pacify the world,

guard well this holy retreat,
and receive us in orthodox faith and repentance,
as a kind and loving Lord.

The power of the Father guide me,
the wisdom of the Son enlighten me,
the working of the Spirit quicken me.

Guard Thou my soul,
strengthen my body,
elevate my senses,
direct my course,
order my habits,
shape my character,
bless my actions,
fulfil my prayers,
inspire holy thoughts,
pardon the past,
correct the present,
prevent the future.

Now unto Him that is able to do
exceeding abundantly above all that we ask or think,
according to the power that worketh in us,
unto Him be glory in the Church by Christ Jesus
throughout all ages, world without end.   Amen.

6. THANKSGIVING.

Blessed, and praised, and celebrated,
and magnified, and exalted, and glorified,
and hallowed,
be Thy name, O Lord,
its record, and its memory,
and every memorial of it,

for the most honourable senate of the patriarchs,
the ever venerable band of the prophets,
the glorious company of the apostles,
the evangelists,
the illustrious army of the martyrs,
the assembly of confessors,
doctors,
ascetics,
the beauty of virgins,
for infants the delight of the world,

for their faith,	their hope,
their labours,	their truth,
their blood,	their zeal,
their diligence,	their tears,
their purity,	their beauty.

Glory to Thee, O Lord, glory to Thee,
glory to Thee Who didst glorify them,
among whom we too glorify Thee.

Great and marvellous are Thy works,
Lord God Almighty;
just and true are Thy ways,
Thou King of saints.

Who shall not fear Thee, O Lord,
and glorify Thy name?
for Thou only art holy:
for all nations shall come and worship
before Thee;
for Thy judgments are made manifest.

Praise our God, all ye His servants,
and ye that fear Him,
both small and great.
Alleluia:

for the Lord God Omnipotent reigneth;
let us be glad and rejoice, and give honour to Him.

Behold, the tabernacle of God is with men,
and He will dwell with them,
and they shall be His people,
and God Himself shall be with them,
and shall wipe away all tears from their eyes;
and there shall be no more death,
neither sorrow, nor crying, neither shall there be
any more pain:
for the former things are passed away.

MORNING PRAYERS

A Prayer on Awaking.

GLORY be to Thee, O Lord, glory to Thee,
      glory to Thee Who gavest me sleep
        to recruit my weakness,
        and to remit the labours
          of this toilful flesh.
      To this day and all days
a perfect, holy, peaceful, healthful, sinless course
                    vouchsafe, O Lord.

The angel of peace, a faithful guide,
         guardian of souls and bodies,
         to encamp round about me,
    and ever to prompt what is for salvation,
                    vouchsafe, O Lord.

Pardon and remission
         of all sins and of all offences
                    vouchsafe, O Lord.

To our souls what is good and profitable,
        and to the world peace,
                    vouchsafe, O Lord.

Repentance and holy fear
        for the residue of our life,
    and health and peace to the end,
                    vouchsafe, O Lord.

Whatsoever things are true, whatsoever things are
honest,
whatsoever things are just, whatsoever things are
pure,
whatsoever things are lovely, whatsoever things
are of good report;
if there be any virtue, if there be any praise,
such thoughts, such deeds,
vouchsafe, O Lord.

A Christian close of life,
without sin, without shame,
and, should it please Thee, without pain,
and a good answer
at the dread and awful judgment seat
of Jesus Christ our Lord,
vouchsafe, O Lord.

Another Prayer on Awaking.

Blessed art Thou, O Lord,
our God,
the God of our fathers;
Who turnest the shadow of death into the morning,
and renewest the face of the earth;
Who rollest away the darkness from before the light,
banishest night, and bringest back the day;
Who lightenest mine eyes,
lest I sleep the sleep of death;
Who deliverest me from the terror by night,
from the pestilence that walketh in darkness;
Who drivest sleep from mine eyes,
and slumber from mine eyelids;
Who makest the outgoings of the morning and
evening to rejoice;

because I laid me down and slept and awaked,
for Thou, Lord, madest me dwell in safety:
because I awaked and beheld,
and my sleep was sweet unto me.

Blot out as the thick cloud of night my transgressions,
and scatter as the morning cloud my sins.
Grant me to be a child of the light, and of the day;
to walk soberly, spotlessly, honestly, as in the day.
Vouchsafe to keep me this day without sin.
Thou Who upholdest the falling and liftest the fallen,
let me not harden my heart in provocation,
or temptation, or in deceitfulness of any sin.

Moreover, deliver me this day
from the snare of the fowler,
and from the noisome pestilence;
from the arrow that flieth by day,
and from the destruction that wasteth at noonday.
Defend this day against my evil,
against the evil of this day defend Thou me.
Let not my days be consumed in vanity,
nor my years in trouble.
Day unto day uttereth speech:
to-day some knowledge, or deed, unto yesterday.

Cause me to hear Thy lovingkindness in the morning;
for in Thee do I trust:
cause me to know the way wherein I should walk;
for I lift up my soul unto Thee.
Deliver me, O Lord, from mine enemies:
I flee unto Thee to hide me.
Teach me to do Thy will; for Thou art my God:
Thy Spirit is good;
lead me into the land of uprightness.

Quicken me, O Lord, for Thy name's sake :
for thy righteousness' sake bring my soul out of trouble.

Remove from my soul thoughts that are without
understanding,
inspire those which are good
and pleasing in Thy sight.
Turn away mine eyes from beholding vanity ;
let mine eyes look right on,
and let mine eyelids look straight before me.
Hedge up mine ears with thorns,
lest they incline to undisciplined words.
Morning by morning, waken Thou mine ear
to hear as the learned.
Set a watch, O Lord, before my mouth :
keep the door of my lips.
Let my speech be seasoned with salt,
that it may minister grace unto the hearers.
Let no deed be grief unto me, nor offence of heart.
Let some work be done
for which Thou wilt remember me, Lord, for good ;
and spare me according to the multitude of Thy
mercy.

Into Thine hand I commit
my spirit, soul, and body,
which Thou hast created, redeemed, regenerated,
O Lord God of truth ;
and, with me, all who are mine,
and all that I have.
Thou hast graciously given them to me,
Lord, in Thy goodness.
Preserve us from all evil,
preserve our souls, I beseech Thee, O Lord ;
keep us from falling,

and present us faultless
before the presence of Thy glory in that day.

Preserve my going out and my coming in
from this time forth, and even for evermore.
Prosper, I pray Thee, Thy servant this day,
and grant him mercy
in the sight of those who meet him.
Make haste, O God, to deliver me ;
make haste to help me, O Lord.

O turn unto me, and have mercy upon me ;
give Thy strength unto Thy servant,
and save the son of Thine handmaid.
Shew me a token for good ;
that they which hate me may see it and be ashamed :
because Thou, Lord, hast holpen me,
and comforted me.

Another Prayer on Awaking.

O THOU that hearest prayer,
unto Thee shall all flesh come.
Evening, and morning, and at noon,
will I pray, and cry aloud :
and Thou shalt hear my voice.
My voice shalt Thou hear in the morning, O Lord ;
in the morning will I direct my prayer unto Thee,
and will look up.
Let my prayer be set forth
before Thee as incense.

I have remembered Thee upon my bed,
and meditated on Thee in the night watches,
because Thou hast been my help.

I give Thee thanks, Almighty Lord, Everlasting God,
for that Thou hast vouchsafed
to preserve me this night,
not according to my deserts,
but according to Thy holy compassion.

Grant unto me, O Lord,
so to pass this day in Thy holy service,
that the submission of my obedience
may be well pleasing unto Thee.
I lift up my heart with my hands unto God
in the heavens.
Behold, as the eyes of servants
look unto the hand of their masters,
and as the eyes of a maiden
unto the hand of her mistress;
so our eyes wait upon the Lord our God,
until that He have mercy upon us.
Look Thou upon me, and be merciful unto me,
as Thou usest to do unto those that love Thy name.

Give Thine angels charge over me,
to keep me in all my ways.
Shew me Thy ways, O Lord; teach me Thy paths.
Order my steps according to Thy word:
and let not any iniquity have dominion over me.
Hold up my goings in Thy paths,
that my footsteps slip not.

Put into my mouth words honest and well chosen;
that my conversation and my countenance,
my walk, and all my works,
may be pleasing unto all men that see and hear me;
that I may find grace in all that I say and seek.

A Confession and Prayer for Grace.

O Thou Lover of men,
Thou that art very pitiful,
the Father of mercies,
rich in mercy to all that call upon Thee,
I have sinned against heaven and in Thy sight,
and am no more worthy to be called Thy son,
nor to be made one of Thy hired servants,
no, not the lowest.

But I repent; woe is me, I repent;
help Thou mine impenitence;
and if there be any comfort of love,
if any bowels and mercies,
by the multitude, by the riches, of Thy grace,
by the exceeding abundance of Thy mercy,
by the great love wherewith Thou hast loved us,
be merciful to me a sinner,
to me of all sinners the greatest,
the most wretched.
Deep calleth unto deep:
the deep of our misery unto the deep of Thy mercy;
where sin hath abounded,
there let grace much more abound;
overcome our evil with Thy good;
let mercy rejoice against judgment.

But above and before all things,
I believe that Thou art the Christ,
the Son of the living God.
Thou Who didst come into the world to save
sinners,

of whom I am chief,
save me.
Thou Who takest away the sin of the world,
take away mine.
Thou Who didst come to redeem the lost,
let not one whom Thou hast redeemed perish.

Deliver me from the recollection of evil things,
that what I have seen and heard
from the wicked, in this world,
I may not remember, nor ever tell to others;
that I may hate every false way.
I have deserved death;
but I appeal from the tribunal of Thy justice
to the throne of Thy grace.

Another Act of Confession.

ESSENCE beyond essence, Nature increate,
Framer of the world,
I set Thee, Lord, before me,
and unto Thee do I lift up my soul.
I worship Thee on my knees,
and humble myself under Thy mighty hand.
I stretch forth my hands unto Thee:
my soul thirsteth after Thee, as a thirsty land.

I smite upon my breast,
and say, with the publican,
God be merciful to me a sinner,
the chief of sinners;
to the sinner above the publican
be merciful, as to the publican.
Father of mercies, I beseech Thy fatherly pity,
despise me not,

an unclean worm, a dead dog, a body of death;
despise not Thou the work of Thine own hands;
despise not Thine own image,
though bearing the brands of sin.
Lord, if Thou wilt, Thou canst make me clean.
Lord, speak the word only, and I shall be healed.

And Thou, my Saviour Christ,
Christ my Saviour,
Saviour of sinners, of whom I am chief,
despise me not; despise me not, O Lord,
who am purchased with Thy blood,
called by Thy name;
but look on me with those eyes
with which Thou didst look upon
Magdalene at the feast,
Peter in the hall,
the thief on the cross:
that with the thief I may entreat Thee humbly,
Lord, remember me when Thou comest
into Thy kingdom;
that with Peter I may weep bitterly and say,
O that mine eyes were a fountain of tears,
that I might weep day and night;
that with Magdalene I may hear Thee say,
Thy sins are forgiven thee,
and with her may love much,
for my sins, which are many and manifold,
are forgiven.

And Thou, all-holy, good, and life-giving Spirit,
despise me not, Thy breath,
despise not Thine own holy things;
but return, O Lord; how long?
and let it repent Thee concerning Thy servant.

An Act of Intercession.

LET us pray for the Catholic Church :
for the Churches throughout the whole world,
for their verity, unity, and stability,
that in all charity may flourish,
and truth may live ;
for our Church :
that what is wanting in it may be supplied,
what is unsound, corrected ;
that all heresies, schisms, scandals,
as well public as private,
may be removed.
Correct the wandering,
convert the unbelieving,
increase the faith of the Church,
destroy heresies,
expose the crafty enemies, weaken the violent.
Pray we for the ministry :
that they may rightly divide,
that they may walk uprightly ;
that, while they teach others, themselves may learn ;

for the people :
that they seek not to be wise above measure ;
but may be persuaded by reason,
and yield to the authority of superiors ;
for governments :
their stability and peace ;
for our kingdom, corporation, city :
that they may fare well and prosperously,
and be freed from all danger and inconvenience ;

for the king :
> save him now, O Lord,
> O Lord, send him now prosperity ;
> crown him with the array of truth and glory ;
> speak good things to his heart
> for Thy Church and people ;

for the prudence of his counsellors,
> the equity and integrity of the judges,
> the courage of the army,
> the temperance of the people,
> and their godly simplicity ;

for the succession :
> whether in universities or in schools,
> that, as they increase in age,
> they may also increase in wisdom, and in favour
> with God and man ;

for them that shew themselves benevolent,
> whether towards the Church,
> or towards the poor and needy :
> reward Thou them sevenfold into their bosom ;
> let their souls dwell at ease,
> and their seed inherit the earth.
> Blessed be they that consider the poor.

That it may please Thee to reward all our benefactors
> with eternal blessings,
> that for their benefits bestowed on us upon earth
> they may obtain everlasting rewards in heaven ;
> that it may please Thee to behold and to relieve
> the miseries of the poor and the captives ;
> that it may please Thee of Thy merciful compassion
> to repair the frail lapses of the flesh,
> and to uphold them that are falling ;
> that it may please Thee graciously to accept
> our reasonable service ;

that it may please Thee to raise our minds
to heavenly desires;
that it may please Thee to regard us
with the eyes of Thy compassion;
that it may please Thee to preserve the souls
of us and ours
from everlasting damnation;
that it may please Thee to grant unto me,
with those for whom I have prayed,
or for whom I am in any way bound to pray,
and with all the people of God,
an entrance into Thy kingdom,
there to behold Thy face in righteousness,
and to be satisfied with Thy likeness:
We beseech Thee to hear us, good Lord.

An Act of Thanksgiving.

ALL Thy works shall praise Thee, O Lord,
and Thy saints shall bless Thee.
It is a good thing to give thanks unto the Lord,
and to sing praises unto Thy name, O Most High:
to shew forth Thy lovingkindness
in the morning,
and Thy faithfulness
every night.
I will extol Thee, my God, O King,
and I will bless Thy name for ever and ever.
Every day will I bless Thee,
and I will praise Thy name for ever and ever,

Who didst call the things that were not,
as though they were;
by Whom all things were made
in heaven and in earth, visible and invisible,

Who upholdest all things by the word of Thy power;
Who dost not leave Thyself without witness,
  in that Thou doest good, and givest us
  rain from heaven, and fruitful seasons,
  filling our hearts with food and gladness;
  in that all things continue this day
  according to Thine ordinances,
  for all are Thy servants;

Who, having before taken counsel,
  didst Thyself, with Thine own hands,
  make man out of the dust of the earth,
and didst breathe into his nostrils the breath of life;
  and didst honour him with Thine image;
  and didst charge Thine angels concerning him;
  and didst set him over the works of Thine hands;
  and didst place him in a paradise of pleasure;
  and didst not despise him, even when he despised
  Thy commandments;
but didst open for him a door unto repentance and life,
giving him Thy exceeding great and precious promise
  concerning the seed of the woman;
Who hast instructed our race,
  by that which may be known of God,
  by that which is written in the law,
  by the rite of sacrifices,
  by the oracles of the prophets,
  by the melody of the psalms,
  by the wisdom of the proverbs,
  by the experience of the histories;

Who, when the fulness of the time was come,
  didst send forth Thy Son,
  Who took on Him the seed of Abraham,
  and made Himself of no reputation,

taking upon Him the form of a servant;
and, being made of a woman, made under the law,
by the offering of His life accomplished its obedience,
by the sacrifice of His death removed its curse,
redeeming our race by His death,
quickening it by His resurrection,
leaving nothing undone, that could be done,
to make us partakers of the divine nature;
and hath manifested in every place
the savour of His knowledge,
by the preaching of the gospel,
bearing Himself witness
with divers signs and wonders,
by singular holiness of life,
by mighty power even unto shedding of blood,
by the marvellous conversion of the world to the faith,
without aid of authority, without help of persuasion;

Who hast made us children of the saints,
and heirs of the same calling;
Who hast granted to Thy Church
that she should be the pillar and ground of the truth,
and that the gates of hell
should not prevail against her;
Who hast granted unto our Church
that she should keep that which was
committed unto her,
and should teach us the way of peace,
and retain order, stability, and decency;

Who hast confirmed the throne of Thy servant,
our king;
Who hast made peace in our borders,
and filled us with the finest of the wheat;
Who hast strengthened the bars of our gates,
and hast blessed our children within us;

Who hast clothed our enemies with shame;
Who hast made us blessed for ever,
   and hast made us exceeding glad with Thy
         countenance;
Who hast instructed our princes,
       and taught our senators wisdom;
Who hast given us pastors according to Thine heart,
 that feed us with knowledge and understanding;
Who hast turned our swords into plowshares,
    and our spears into pruninghooks;
Who hast caused that there should be no breaking in,
   nor going out, and no complaining
      in our streets;

Who didst bring me forth into this life,
 and didst bring me to the washing of regeneration,
   and renewing of the Holy Ghost;
   and hast made known to me Thy ways;
   and hast overlooked my sins, because
     I should amend;
   and hast not consumed me by the hand of
     mine iniquity,
  but hast waited to shew mercy upon me;
Who hast not suffered my heart to be hardened,
   but hast left me compunction of soul,
    remembrance of my latter end,
    conscience of sins committed;
   and to me confessing and imploring
    hast opened a door of hope,
through the power of Thy mysteries and the keys;
Who hast not cut off like a weaver my life,
 nor from day even to night made an end of me,
  nor taken me away in the midst of my days,
   but hast holden my soul in life,
   and suffered not my feet to be moved.

EVENING PRAYERS

Meditations before Evening Prayer.

In war there is the note of charge, fitted for the onset : of recall, whereby stragglers are recalled ;

And the mind of man, as it must be stirred up in the morning, so in the evening, as by a note of recall, is it to be called back to itself and to its Leader by a scrutiny and inquisition or examination of self, by prayers and thanksgivings.

A good man would rather know his infirmity, than the foundations of the earth, or the heights of the heavens.

But that knowledge of our own infirmity is not attained save by diligent inquisition, without which the mind is for the most part blind, and sees nothing of that which pertains to it.

There are many hiding places and recesses in the mind.

You must come to the knowledge of, before you can amend, yourself.

An ulcer unknown grows worse and worse, and is deprived of cure.

The heart is deceitful above all things.

The old man is bound up in a thousand folds.

Therefore take heed to thyself.

This chiefly is to be inquired :

What hast thou to-day
{
done, read,
said, written,
that
{
befits a Christian, a priest, a father, etc.
may confirm faith, obedience.
may increase knowledge,
the good government of mind, of body.
may work out the salvation of thyself, of others.
}
}

We see that God Himself concluded each day of the old creation in no other manner than by a review of the works of each, and he saw that all were good.

Cato exacted of himself an account of every day's business, and so also Pythagoras.

Ausonius from Pythagoras :

Nor let sweet sleep upon thine eyes descend,
Till thou hast judged its deeds at each day's end.

King David, when the day was over, communed with his own heart, and his spirit made diligent search.

In this Areopagitic nightly examination, see that thou shew thyself the judge, not the patron, of thy sins ; and say in the tribunal of thy mind, say with grief and indignation : I acknowledge my transgressions, O Lord ; who will set scourges over my thoughts, and the discipline of wisdom over mine heart ?

If we judged ourselves, we should not be judged.

Prayer is the guardian of the sleeping, the confidence of the waking.

We think him not safe who is undefended by the arms and the guard of prayer.

Rightly therefore teacheth Rabbi Jarchi that penitence must not be put off till the morrow.

Behold the hope of fruit and eternal salvation shall have deceived itself for ever, unless even in this very night thou shalt have freed thy soul.

And if an examination of this kind takes place for some days, or at farthest one month, with penitence, it will suffice to form a perfect habit of virtue.

A Prayer for Grace.

THE day is gone,
and I give Thee thanks, O Lord.
Evening draws nigh;
make it bright.
As day has its evening,
so also has life:
the evening of life is age;
age has overtaken me,
make it bright.
Cast me not off in the time of old age;
forsake me not when my strength faileth.
Even to my old age be Thou He,
and even to hoar hairs carry me;
do Thou make, do Thou bear,
do Thou carry and deliver me.
Abide with me, Lord,
for it is toward evening,
and the day is far spent
of this toilful life.
Let Thy strength be made perfect
in my weakness.

The day is fled and gone;
life too is going,
this lifeless life.
Night cometh;
and cometh death,
the deathless death.
As the end of the day is near,
so too is the end of life;
we then, also remembering it,
beseech of Thee,

for the close of our life,
that Thou wouldest guide it in peace
to be Christian, acceptable, sinless, shameless,
and, should it please Thee, painless,
Lord, O Lord, gathering us together
under the feet of Thy chosen,
when Thou wilt, and as Thou wilt,
only without shame and sin.
Let us remember the days of darkness,
for they are many,
lest we be cast into outer darkness.
Let us remember to outstrip the night,
doing some good thing.

Near is judgment;
a good and acceptable answer
at the dread and awful judgment seat
of Jesus Christ
vouchsafe to us, O Lord.

An Act of Thanksgiving.

By night I lift up my hands in the sanctuary,
and bless the Lord.
The Lord hath commanded His lovingkindness
in the daytime,
and in the night His song shall be with me
and my prayer unto the God of my life.
I will bless Thee while I live,
and lift up my hands in Thy name.
Let my prayer be set forth before Thee as incense;
and the lifting up of my hands
as the evening sacrifice.
Blessed art Thou, O Lord, our God,
the God of our fathers,

Who hast ordained the changes of day and night,
Who givest songs in the night,
Who hast delivered us from the evil of this day,
Who hast not cut off like a weaver my life,
nor from day even to night made an end of me.

An Act of Confession and Prayer for Grace.

Lord, as we add day to day, so sin to sin.
The just falleth seven times a day,
and I, an exceeding sinner,
fall seventy times seven:
a wonderful, a horrible thing, O Lord.
But I turn back with groans
from my evil ways,
and I return to my own heart,
and with all my heart I return to Thee.

O God of penitents and Saviour of sinners,
evening by evening I will return
in the innermost marrow of my soul;
and my soul out of the depths crieth unto Thee:
I have sinned, O Lord, I have sinned
grievously against Thee;
alas, alas, woe is me for my misery.
I repent, O me, I repent; spare me, O Lord;
I repent, O me, I repent;
help Thou my impenitence.

Spare me, O Lord; be merciful unto me;
I said, Lord, be merciful unto me,
heal my soul, for I have sinned against Thee.
Have mercy upon me, O Lord,

according to Thy lovingkindness,
according to the multitude of Thy tender mercies
blot out my transgressions.

Remit the guilt,
heal the wound,
blot out the stains, deliver from the shame,
rescue from the tyranny,
and make me not a public example.

O bring Thou me out of my distresses,
cleanse Thou me from secret faults,
keep back Thy servant also from presumptuous sins.
My wanderings of mind and idle talking
lay not to my charge.
Remove the dark and muddy flood
of foul and lawless thoughts.

O Lord, I have destroyed myself;
whatever I have done amiss, mercifully pardon.
Deal not with us after our sins,
nor reward us according to our iniquities.
Look mercifully upon our infirmities;
and, for the glory of Thy all-holy name,
turn from us all those ills and miseries
which by our sins, and by us through them,
are most righteously and worthily deserved.

An Act of Commendation.

To my weariness, O Lord,
vouchsafe Thou rest;
to my exhaustion
renew Thou strength.

Lighten mine eyes, lest I sleep the sleep of death.
Deliver me from the terror by night,
from the pestilence that walketh in darkness.
Give me sound sleep,
and to pass this night without fear.

O Keeper of Israel,
Who neither slumberest nor sleepest,
preserve me this night from all evil,
preserve my soul.
Visit me with the visitation of Thine own,
reveal to me wisdom in the visions of the night.
If not, for I am not worthy, not worthy,
at least, O sovereign Lord, O Lover of men,
let sleep be to me a breathing time,
as from toil, so from sin.

Yea, O Lord, nor let me in my dreams imagine
what may anger Thee, what may defile me.
Let not my loins be filled with illusions;
nay rather, let my reins instruct me
in the night season,
yet without grievous terror.
Preserve me from the black sleep of sin;
every earthly and evil thought put to sleep within me.

Grant to me light sleep,
rid of all imaginations fleshly and satanical.

Lord, Thou, Who madest me, knowest
how sleepless are mine unseen foes,
and how feeble my wretched flesh.

Let the wing of Thy pity shelter me;
awaken me at the fitting time, the time of prayer;

and give me to seek Thee early,
in praise of Thy glory,
and for Thy service.

Into Thine hand, O Lord, I commit myself,
my spirit, soul, and body :
Thou didst make, and didst redeem them ;
and, together with me, all my friends,
and all that is mine.
Thou hast graciously given them to me, Lord,
in Thy goodness.

Guard my downsitting and mine uprising,
from this time forth and even for evermore.
Let me remember Thee upon my bed,
and let my spirit make diligent search ;
let me awake and be still with Thee.

I will both lay me down in peace, and sleep :
for Thou, Lord, only
makest me dwell in safety.

MEDITATIONS AND PRAYERS
FOR VARIOUS TIMES
AND SEASONS

An Horology.

O Thou, Who hast put in Thine own power
the times and the seasons:
give us grace that in a fitting
and acceptable time we may pray unto Thee;
and deliver us.
Thou, Who for us men and for our salvation
wast born in the depth of night:
grant us to be born again daily
by renewing of the Holy Ghost,
until Christ Himself be formed in us,
to a perfect man;
and deliver us.
Thou, Who very early in the morning,
at the rising of the sun,
didst rise again from the dead:
raise us also daily to newness of life,
suggesting to us, for Thou knowest them,
frames of repentance;
and deliver us.
Thou, Who at the third hour didst send down
Thy Holy Spirit
on the apostles:
take not the same Holy Spirit from us,
but renew Him daily in our hearts;
and deliver us.
Thou, Who at the sixth hour of the sixth day
didst nail together with Thyself upon the cross
the sins of the world:

blot out the handwriting of our sins
that is against us;
and, taking it away, deliver us.
Thou, Who at the sixth hour didst let down
a great sheet from heaven to earth,
the symbol of Thy Church:
receive into it us sinners of the Gentiles,
and with it receive us up into heaven;
and deliver us.
Thou, Who at the seventh hour didst command
the fever to leave the nobleman's son:
if there be any fever in our hearts,
if any sickness, remove it from us also;
and deliver us.
Thou, Who at the ninth hour for us sinners
and for our sins
didst taste of death:
mortify in us our members which are upon the earth,
and whatsoever is contrary to Thy will;
and deliver us.
Thou, Who didst will the ninth hour to be
the hour of prayer:
hear us while we pray at the hour of prayer,
and grant unto us that which we pray for and
desire;
and deliver us.
Thou, Who at the tenth hour didst grant unto
Thine apostle
to discover Thy Son,
and to cry out with great gladness,
We have found the Messiah:
grant unto us also, in like manner,
to find the same Messiah,
and, having found Him, to rejoice in like manner;
and deliver us.

Thou, Who didst, even at the eleventh hour of the
day,
of Thy goodness send into Thy vineyard
those that had stood all the day idle,
promising them a reward :
grant unto us the like grace,
and, though it be late,
even as it were about the eleventh hour,
favourably receive us who return unto Thee ;
and deliver us.

Thou, Who at the sacred hour of the supper
wast pleased to institute
the mysteries of Thy body and blood :
render us mindful and partakers of the same,
yet never to condemnation, but to the remission
of sin,
and to the obtaining of the promises
of the new testament ;
and deliver us.

Thou, Who at eventide wast pleased to be taken down
from the cross,
and laid in the grave :
take away from us, and bury in Thy sepulchre,
our sins,
covering whatever evil we have committed
with good works ;
and deliver us.

Thou, Who late in the night, by breathing
on Thine apostles,
didst bestow on them the power
of the remission and retention of sins :
grant unto us to experience that power
for their remission, O Lord,
not for their retention ;
and deliver us.

Thou, Who at midnight didst raise David Thy prophet,
and Paul Thine apostle, that they should praise
Thee :
give us also songs in the night,
and to remember Thee upon our beds ;
and deliver us.
Thou, Who with Thine own mouth hast declared,
at midnight the Bridegroom shall come :
grant that the cry may ever sound in our ears,
Behold, the Bridegroom cometh,
that we may never be unprepared to go forth
to meet Him ;
and deliver us.
Thou, Who by the crowing of the cock,
didst admonish Thine apostle,
and didst cause him to return to repentance :
grant that we, at the same warning, may follow his
example,
may go forth and weep bitterly
for the things in which we have sinned against Thee ;
and deliver us.
Thou, Who hast foretold Thy coming to judgment
in a day when we think not, and in an hour
when we are not aware :
grant that every day and every hour
we may be prepared, and waiting Thy advent ;
and deliver us.

Thou, Who sendest forth the light,
and createst the morning,
and makest Thy sun to rise on the evil
and on the good :
enlighten the blindness of our minds by the
knowledge of the truth,
lift Thou up the light of Thy countenance upon us,

that in Thy light we may see light,
and at length in the light of grace the light of glory.
Thou, Who givest food to all flesh,
Who feedest the young ravens which cry unto Thee,
and hast held us up from our youth until now,
fill our hearts with food and gladness,
and stablish our hearts with Thy grace.

Thou, Who hast made the evening the end
of the day,
so that Thou mightest bring the evening of life
to our minds :
grant us always to consider
that our life passeth away like a day ;
to remember the days of darkness,
that they are many,
that the night cometh wherein no man can work ;
by good works to prevent the darkness,
lest we be cast out into outer darkness ;
and continually to cry unto Thee,
Abide with us, Lord,
for it is toward evening, and the day of our life
is far spent.

The work of the Creator is justice ;
of the Redeemer, mercy ;
of the Holy Ghost, inspiration,
Who is the other Comforter,
the Anointing,
the Seal,
the Earnest.

An Act of Confession.

Two things I recognise, O Lord, in myself :
nature, which Thou hast made,
sin, which I have added.
I confess that by sin I have depraved nature ;
but remember Thou that I am but a wind
that passeth away, and returneth not again,
for of myself I cannot return again from sin.
Take away from me that which I have made ;
let that remain in me which Thou hast made,
that what Thou hast redeemed
with Thy precious blood perish not.
Let not my wickedness destroy
what Thy goodness hath redeemed.

O Lord my God, if I have been able so to do
as to become Thy culprit,
can I have been able so to do
as to cease to be Thy servant ?
If by my sin I have destroyed my innocence,
have I also by my sin destroyed Thy mercy ?
If I have committed that for which
Thou mightest condemn me,
hast Thou at all lost that by which
Thou art wont to save ?
Truth, Lord : in my own conscience
I deserve damnation,
but no offence is so great as Thy compassion.

Spare me therefore,
because it is not difficult to Thy power,
nor unbefitting Thy justice,

nor unwonted to Thy mercy,
to spare the sinner.
Thou Who hast created me, do not destroy me;
Thou Who hast redeemed me, do not condemn me.
Thou Who hast created me
by Thy goodness,
let not Thy work come to nought
through my iniquity.
What is Thine in me, acknowledge;
what is mine, take away.

Look on me, the wretched,
O boundless Lovingkindness:
on me, the wicked,
O Compassion that extendest to all.
Infirm, I come to the Almighty,
wounded, I hasten to the Physician:
reserve for me the gentleness
of Thy compassion,
Who hast so long held suspended the sword
of Thy vengeance.

Blot out the number of my crimes,
renew the multitude of Thy tender mercies.
However unclean, Thou canst cleanse me;
however blind, Thou canst enlighten me;
however weak, Thou canst restore me;
yea, though dead, Thou canst raise me.

Of what kind soever I am, be it good or bad,
I am ever Thine.
If Thou cast me out, who shall take me in?
If Thou disregard me, who shall look on me?
More canst Thou remit, than I commit;
more canst Thou spare, than I offend.

Let not harmful pleasure overcome me,
let not any perverse habit overwhelm me ;
preserve me from depraved and lawless desires,
from vain, hurtful, impure imaginations,
from the illusions of evil spirits,
from pollutions of mind and of body.

Another Act of Confession.

O God, Thou knowest my foolishness,
and my sins are not hid from Thee.
I acknowledge my transgressions, and my sin is
ever before me.
I cover not my transgressions, like Adam ;
nor do I incline my heart to words of wickedness,
to make excuses for my sins.
I will confess my transgressions unto the Lord,
and all that is within me and all my bones shall say,
I have sinned, I have sinned against Thee ;
I have gone astray, like a sheep that is lost ;
I have been perverse, as a bullock unaccustomed
to the yoke ;
I have returned to folly as a dog returneth to
his vomit :
as a sow that was washed to her wallowing
in the mire.
I give glory to Thee, Lord, and make confession
that I have sinned ; and thus and thus have I
done.

Lord, break not the bruised reed ;
quench not the smoking flax ;
let not the waterflood overflow me,
neither let the deep swallow me up,
and let not the pit shut her mouth upon me.

Lord, all my desire is before Thee,
  and my groaning is not hid from Thee.
Thou knowest, Lord, that I say the truth
    in Christ, and lie not,
  my conscience also bearing me witness
    in the Holy Ghost,
  that I have great heaviness and continual
    sorrow in my heart,
    because I have thus sinned against Thee;
  that I am a burden to myself, in that I cannot
    sorrow more;
  that I beseech from Thee a contrite heart,
    groanings that cannot be uttered,
    tears of blood.
Woe is me for my leanness,
  for the hardness of my heart,
  for the dryness of my eyes.
Lord, I repent; I repent, O Lord;
  help Thou mine impenitence,
  and more and still more bruise, and wound, and
    pierce, and strike my heart.

  Behold, O Lord,
  that I am indignant with myself
on account of the foolish and vain and mischievous
    and perilous desires of my flesh;
that I abhor myself for the madness and baseness
    and vileness of those desires,
  worthy of confusion and reproach;
  that my confusion is continually before me,
    and the shame of my face hath covered me.
Woe is me, that I did not reverence nor dread
  the incomprehensibleness of the Glory,
  the tremendous Power,
  the awfulness of the Presence,

the strict Justice,
the gentle Goodness.
How have I been drawn away by mine own
lusts;
how have I hated reproof,
and have not obeyed the voice of my teachers.

Behold, O Lord,
that fearfulness and trembling are come upon me,
and the terrors of death are fallen upon me.
What fear, what trembling, what terror,
what agony, what extremity have I yet to see;
what confusion will seize me;
what shades will surround me.
How terrible is Thy judgment seat, O God,
when the thrones are set and the angels in
presence,
and men brought in, and the books opened,
and the works investigated,
and the thoughts scrutinised,
and the hidden things of darkness made
known.
What will be the judgment against me?
when there is the incorruptible Judge,
and the tremendous tribunal,
and the excuseless defence,
and the irrefragable accusation,
and the fearful punishment, and the eternal
Gehenna,
and the pitiless angels, and the open hell-mouth,
and the roaring river of fire, and that fire
inextinguishable,
and the prison of darkness, and that darkness
rayless,
and the bed of live coals, and the restless worm,

and the indissoluble chains, and the immeasurable
    chaos,
and the wall that cannot be passed, and the
    lament that cannot be consoled,
    and none to assist, to advocate, to free.

    Behold, O Lord,
I adjudge myself worthy of, and amenable to,
                and guilty of,
    eternal punishment,
    yea, and all the straits of this world.
From Thee, O Lord, I have merited death, from
    Thee, the Just One ;
but yet to Thee, O Lord, I appeal, to Thee the
    Merciful One :
    from the tribunal of justice to the mercy seat
        of grace ;
    permit, O Lord, this appeal ;
    if Thou dost not, we perish.
        And, O Lord, carest Thou not that we perish?
    Thou Who wilt have all men to be saved,
        Who art not willing that any should perish.

    Behold me, O Lord,
    self-condemned.
    Behold me ; and enter not Thou, O Lord, into
        judgment with Thy servant.
I am less than the least of all Thy mercies ;
I am not worthy to be made even the lowest of
        Thy hired servants ;
I am not worthy to gather the crumbs that fall
        from Thy table ;
I am not worthy to touch the hem of Thy garment.
        And now, O Lord, humbling myself under
        Thy mighty hand,

I bow my knees to Thee, and fall down to the
ground, on my face.
I stretch forth my hands unto Thee ;
my soul thirsteth after Thee, as a thirsty land.
I dare not lift up so much as
mine eyes unto heaven,
but smite upon my breast.
Out of the depths hath my soul cried unto Thee,
and all that is within me.

For Thy great mercy, for the multitude of Thy
tender mercies,
for Thy name's sake, for the glory of Thy name,
be merciful to my sin ;
for it is great, it is exceeding great.
For the multitude, the great multitude, the riches,
the abundance, the superabundance
of Thy tender mercies,
be merciful unto me, O Lord, a sinner :
Lord, O Lord, be merciful unto me, chief of sinners.
Lord, let Thy mercy rejoice against Thy judgment,
in my sin.
O my Lord, where my sin hath abounded, there let
Thy grace more exceedingly abound.
O Lord, hear; O Lord, forgive; O Lord, hearken, and do;
defer not, for Thine own sake, O my God.

A Confession of Faith.

I believe that, for a great mystery of godliness,
for us men, and for our salvation, Jesus the Man,
the Son of the Father, the Anointed of the Spirit,
our Lord, both as Creator and Redeemer,
was God manifested in the flesh ;
that He worketh effectually and manifestly,

by enlightenment of knowledge, and infusion of grace,
    in rebuke, and doctrine, and longsuffering,
    and assistance, and witnessing, and consolation,
        the gifts and fruits of the Spirit.
Give me grace unceasingly to return thanks
    to Thy Word and only Son,
    as the Purifier of our nature, in His conception
            and nativity,
    the Deliverer of our persons, in His sufferings,
            cross, and death,
    the Conqueror of hell, in His descent,
        of death, in His resurrection,
    our Forerunner, in His ascension,
    our Advocate, in His sitting,
    the Perfecter of our faith, in His second advent ;
Who to our destroyer opposes Himself as our Saviour,
    to Abaddon, as Jesus,
    to Satan, the adversary, as our Mediator,
    to the Devil, the calumniator, as our Advocate,
    to the accuser, as our Intercessor,
        to him that leadeth us captive, as our Redeemer.

A Prayer for Grace.

GRANT that Christ Himself may be formed in us,
    that we may be made conformable to His image ;
    when I am lukewarm in prayer, and stand in need
    of any grace, or heavenly consolation, may I re-
    member Thy sitting, to appear and intercede for
    us; when I am inflamed by passion and evil desire,
    may I never forget Thy dread judgment seat, and
    may the last trump ceaselessly sound in mine ears.
For Thine Anointed's sake, O Father, Who anointest,
grant that we may receive from Thee Thine anointing,

the grace that bringeth salvation, Thy unspeakable
gift of the Holy Spirit,
in saving compunction, in clearness of knowledge,
in fervent prayer, in love shed abroad,
in the witness of the seal and of the earnest;
that I may never quench the Spirit,
nor strive against Him, nor grieve Him,
nor do Him despite, O Lord.

Grant that we may be called in Thy Church,
may be living members thereof in wish and will,
as it is Catholic,
and may be partakers, as it is holy, in its communion
of holy things and persons, holy prayers and service,
unto assurance of the remission of sins,
and the hope of resurrection and translation
unto life eternal.
Lord, increase my faith as a grain of mustard seed.
Let it not be dead, nor temporary, nor feigned;
but a faith that worketh through love, and by
deeds, that ministers to virtue, and conquers the
world, a faith most holy.

An Act of Intercession.

O GOD of truth, the Prince of peace,
let there be peace and truth in our days;
let all that believe be of one heart and of one soul.
O Thou Who breakest not the bruised reed,
Who quenchest not the smoking flax,
establish all them that stand in truth and grace,
restore them that are falling through error or sin.
I beseech Thee, O Lord, of Thy mercy,
let Thine anger be turned away from this city,
and from this house;

for we have sinned against Thee.
Be Thou pleased favourably to regard this place and
all this land, tempering justice with mercy.

Grant that I may love them that love me, even
though unknown to me ;
and bring them, as me, into Thy heavenly kingdom ;
and grant that I may shew them the mercy of God,
by remembering them in my prayers ;
that I, with those for whom I have prayed,
and those for whom I am in any way bound to pray,
and with all the people of God,
may have an entrance into Thy kingdom,
there to appear in righteousness, and to be satisfied
with glory.

An Act of Thanksgiving.

BLESSED is the people that know the joyful sound :
they shall walk, O Lord, in the light of Thy
countenance.
In Thy name shall they rejoice all the day :
and in Thy righteousness shall they be exalted.
My mouth shall speak the praise of the Lord :
and let all flesh bless His holy name for ever
and ever.
O magnify the Lord with me,
and let us exalt His name together.
Come and hear, all ye that fear God ;
and I will declare what He hath done for my soul.

Be Thou exalted, O God, above the heavens ;
let Thy glory be above all the earth.
I will praise the Lord with my whole heart,

in the assembly of the upright, and in the
congregation.
Open Thou my lips; and my mouth shall shew
forth Thy praise.
I will praise Thee with my whole heart:
before the gods will I sing praise unto Thee.
Accept the praises which I, an unworthy sinner,
verily unworthy, yearn to sing:
O that they were devout and acceptable to Thee.
Thou art worthy, Lord God, to receive them;
Thou art my God, and I will praise Thee:
Thou art my God, I will exalt Thee.
I will sing unto the Lord as long as I live:
I will sing praise to my God while I have my being.

Glory to God in the highest,
and on earth peace, good will toward men.
Glory and blessing, strength and power,
honour and thanksgiving, riches and holiness,
praise and wisdom, power and salvation,
be to our God that liveth for ever,
that sitteth upon the throne,
and to the Lamb that was slain.
Amen: Hallelujah.
Hosanna in the highest: blessed is He
that cometh in the name of the Lord.

Another Act of Confession.

BEHOLD me, O Lord, behold me, the greatest, the
worst, the most wretched of sinners. And what
shall I now say, or in what shall I open my
mouth? What shall I answer, when I am guilty,
guilty, guilty? I will go over my sins unto Thee in

the bitterness of my soul; O that it may be in its bitterest bitterness! Behold, for my peace I had great bitterness. O Lord, if by these things men live, and if in all these things is the life of my spirit, so wilt Thou recover me, and make me to live. Like a crane or a swallow, so will I lament: I will mourn as a dove. I beseech Thee, O Lord, by all Thy mercy, let Thy most righteous indignation and fury be turned away from me, because I have sinned, and that grievously. I have sinned against Thee, most often and grievously have I sinned against Thee.

O Father of mercies, I beseech Thy fatherly loving-kindness, despise not an unclean worm, a dead dog, a body of death: despise not me. Yea rather regard me, O Lord, regard me with those eyes wherewith Thou didst regard Magdalene in the banquet, Peter in the hall, the thief on the cross; that with Peter I may weep, with the thief may confess, with Magdalene may love, may love Thee much, yea very much, as one to whom many sins are forgiven. Spare me, O Lord; spare me, a penitent, at the least desiring to be a penitent, and preparing thereto, recollecting my sins with bitterness, indignant with myself concerning them, remembering and laying hold of Thy most bitter passion. Spare, O Lord; have mercy. Spare me, O Lord; have mercy on me; pity me, because it is not difficult to Thy power, nor unbefitting Thy justice, nor unwonted to Thy clemency. That I should thus, for leeks and garlick, have left the bread of angels: that I should thus, for the husks of swine, have despised my Father's table: O wretched, frenzied me! Who bewitched me to such foolishness? O that Thou wouldst deign to receive me again! My mind is wholly to return: better was it with me then, than now. Full therefore of confusion, unworthy to name, or invoke, or think upon Thy name, were it not for Thine own proper goodness, yet relying on that very goodness, suppliant, humble, prostrate, I return to Thee; nor ask I for any thing, but that which Thou hast bestowed most often, and bestowest most willingly; which unless Thou wert again and again to bestow, no flesh could abide, none could stand. Have mercy on me a sinner, the greatest of sinners, and for that very reason needing the greatest mercy. And Thy mercy is the greatest: it reacheth to the heaven above, it freeth from the lowest hell: it is marvellous. Magnify Thy mercy towards me; if Thou seekest to glorify it infinitely, extend it to me; at no time, in no place, hath it been, will it be, more glorious in the pardon of any sinner. If Thou willest, Lord, that I should leave Thee, give me another Thyself; else I will not give Thee up. Let the Spirit of truth lead me into truth.

To Thee, O Lord, I confess, because, if I would, I cannot conceal: to Thee my very many, my very great, my very heinous sins. I profess also to grieve, as Thou knowest. But I need more grief: I plainly need it. I am far from that which I ought to have. I can sin much; I cannot repent much. Woe is me for my dryness, my dryness; I cannot much: I would much. I know that even much is not enough. Would that I had such grief, or even more; but of myself I cannot obtain it: I am dried up, I am dried up like a potsherd: woe is me. Thou, O Lord, increase the fountain of tears that I have; supply that I have not; give me a molten heart, unutterable groans.   Meanwhile, since my mind is willing, accept me according to that I have, not according to that I have not.   I will prolong it, since I cannot increase it, through all the years of my life. After so many backslidings, with what confidence can I now return?   With none.   Altogether confused, altogether covered with confusion, I walk, I sit, I lie down.   Nor should I dare to do it, nor could I do aught but despair, and act like the desperate, unless there were yet a hope left. And what hope?   That Thou wilt extend Thy mercy to seventy times seven.   That measure of forgiveness Thou hast enjoined to us.   Hast thou enjoined this to us, and wilt not Thou Thyself practise the same?   Yea, and much more.   That be far from Thee, that Thou shouldst require more perfection in us than existeth in Thyself: that we must forgive until seventy times seven, but Thou wilt not forgive.   For Thy mercy surpasseth ours, as far as Thyself surpassest us.   I then, trusting in Thy mercy, that forgiveth at the least seventy times seven, stand afar off; and lowlily, as I ought, and most humbly smiting upon my breast, say and repeat, again and again, God have mercy on me a sinner, on me a most wretched sinner, on me the chief of sinners, on me who am altogether sin, on me, who am a very hyperbole of sin, O Thou to Whom prayer can never be made without a hope of pardon.

Shall God forgive, and thou not repent?   God forbid.   I do in a sort repent; I fear me, not sufficiently.   I would that it were more: I should rejoice, were it more; I grieve that it is no more. For I wish that I could more, and grieve that I can no more. I confess that my very grief is to be lamented; and I grieve that it is thus to be lamented. And who will give me to lament it more? I would do so, were it in my power; but it is not. It is in my power to know that I ought, to wish that I did: to will is present with me; but how to perform that which is good, I find not.

Do Thou, O Lord, give me power; if Thou wilt, Thou canst: Thou canst turn even the hard rock into a pool. Give tears, give a fountain of waters to my head. Give the grace of tears. Drop down, ye heavens, from above, and bedew the dryness of my desert heart. Give me, O Lord, this grace. None were more welcome to me; neither riches, nor all the good things of this world were to be coveted in comparison of tears: tears, such as Thou didst give David of old, or Jeremiah, or Peter, or Magdalene. At least give me a dropping eye; let me not altogether be a flint. If I may not water my couch, nor wash Thy feet; if I may not weep bitterly as Peter, plentifully as Jeremiah (and yet, O that it might be even thus), give me at least one or two little tears which Thou mayest put into Thy bottle and write in Thy book. But if I cannot gain this much, woe is me, I am like a pumice, like very lime, fervent in cold water; careless of my state where I least ought to be so; mourning enough, when there is no occasion; cold, arid, dead, where there is the greatest.

At least give me some of the tears of Christ, which He shed plentifully in the days of His flesh. Bestow on me from that store; in Him there is superfluity for my deficiency.

An Act of Deprecation.

O Lord, Thou knowest, and canst, and willest
     the good of my soul.
O wretched man that I am:
    I neither know, nor can, nor, as I ought, will it.

Thou, O Lord, I beseech Thee,
    in Thine unspeakable love,
so order concerning me, and so dispose,
as Thou knowest to be most pleasing to Thee
    and most good for me.

Thine is goodness, grace, love,
    kindness, benignity, gentleness,
forbearance, longsuffering, abundant mercy,
    a multitude of tender mercies,
    a heart of compassion.
The Lord is very pitiful in passing by,
    in overlooking, holding His peace,
many times delivering, many years forbearing;
    He doth not afflict willingly,
    nor stir up all His wrath,
nor reward us according to our iniquities;
    in wrath He remembereth mercy,
    He repenteth Him of the evil.
He rendereth double for all our sins;
    He is ready to pardon,
    to be reconciled,
    to be propitiated.

Another Act of Deprecation.

FATHER, the Creator,
Son, the Redeemer,
Spirit, the Regenerator,
destroy not me,
whom Thou hast created, redeemed, regenerated.
Remember not, Lord, my sins,
nor the sins of my forefathers;
take not vengeance for our sins, theirs and mine.
Spare us, Lord, them and me.
Spare Thy people,
and, among Thy people, Thy servant,
who is redeemed with Thy precious blood;
and be not angry with us for ever.
Be merciful, be merciful; spare us, O Lord;
and be not angry with us for ever.
Be merciful, be merciful; have pity on us, O Lord;
and be not angry with us to the full.

Deal not, O Lord,
deal not with me after my sins,
neither reward me according to mine iniquities;
but after Thy great pity deal with me,
and according to the multitude of Thy mercies
reward me;
after that great pity,
and according to that multitude of mercies,
which Thou shewedst to our fathers
in the times of old.
By all that is dear unto Thee,

from all evil and adversity
in all time of need,
from this evil and this adversity
in this time,
raise me, rescue me, save me, O Lord;
deliver me, O Lord, and destroy me not.

On the bed of sickness,
in the hour of death,
in the day of judgment,
in that dread and awful day,
rescue me, Lord, and save me
from seeing the Judge's face wrathful,
from being placed on the left hand,
from hearing the dreadful word, Depart from Me,
from being bound in chains of darkness,
from being cast into outer darkness,
from being tormented with fire and brimstone,
where the smoke of their torment
ascendeth up for ever and ever.
Be merciful, be merciful,
spare us, pity us,
deliver and save us, O Lord;
and destroy us not for ever.

Let it not be, O Lord;
and, that it be not,
take away from me
hardness of heart,
insensibility after sinning,
blindness of heart,
contempt of Thy warning,
a seared conscience,
a reprobate mind,
the sin against the Holy Ghost,

the sin unto death,
the sins which forerun
the sin against the Holy Ghost.

Deliver me
from all evils and troubles of this world :
from plague, famine, war, earthquake, flood, and fire ;
the stroke of immoderate rain and drought,
blast and blight, thunder, lightning, and tempest ;
sickness, epidemic and malignant,
and sudden death.

Deliver me
from ills and perplexities in the Church :
from private interpretation,
from innovation in things sacred,
from heterodox teaching ;
from unhealthy inquiries and interminable disputes ;
from heresies, schisms, scandals, public or private ;
from making gods of kings,
from flattering the people,
from the indifference of Saul,
from the scorn of Michal,
from the greed of Hophni,
from the usurpation of Athaliah,
from the priesthood of Micah,
from the fraternity of Simon and Judas,
from the doctrine of men unlearned and unstable,
from the pride of novices,
from people as they that strive with the priest.

Deliver me
from anarchy, multitude of rulers, tyranny ;
from Asshur, Jeroboam, Rehoboam, Gallio, Haman,
the profligate counsel of Ahithophel,

the no counsel of them of Zoan,
the statutes of Omri,
the judgments of Jezreel,
the excesses of Belial,
the plague of Peor,
the valley of Achor,
pollution of blood or seed,
incursion of enemies, civil war,
bereavement of good and noble governors,
accession of the wicked and base.

Deliver me
from an insupportable life
in despondency, sickness, evil report,
distress, peril, slavery, tumult;
from death in sin, shame, torture, despair, defilement,
by violence, by treachery:
from death sudden, from death eternal.

Give us help from trouble:
for vain is the help of man.

Another Act of Deprecation.

Look down, O Lord our God, from heaven,
from the habitation of Thy holiness and of
Thy glory.
Thou, Who dwellest on high, yet hast respect
unto the lowly,
look down upon us, and destroy us not;
but deliver us from evil.
From all evil and misfortune deliver us.
As Thou didst deliver our fathers in the times of old,
deliver us.

By whatsoever is dear to Thee, or beloved by Thee,
deliver us.
In all our straits deliver us.

From the evils of the future state,
from Thine anger,
but yet more from Thy ceasing to be angry,
from everlasting damnation,
from all the terrors of the world to come,
from the wrathful countenance of the Judge,
from being placed on the left hand,
from the hearing of that dread and terrible
word, Depart from Me,
from being cast into outer darkness,
from everlasting chains under darkness,
from fire and brimstone,
where the smoke of their torment ascendeth up
for ever and ever, deliver us.
Spare us, O Lord. Have mercy upon us.
Deliver us; and let us never be confounded.

From spiritual evils:
from blindness and hardness of heart,
which lead to impenitence,
from wantonness and from stubbornness,
from a seared conscience,
and from being past feeling after sin,
from a reprobate mind,
from contempt of Thy threatenings,
from the sin unto death,
from the sin against the Holy Ghost,
have mercy upon us, and deliver us, O Lord;
that I be not parched among the tares and stubble,
nor grieve among those that are on the left hand,
nor wither in the tempest,

nor lament in the fire that is never quenched,
nor be condemned to the flames,
nor suffer shame in Gehenna,
nor waste away among the overflowings of Belial,
nor weep in the chains of darkness,
nor gnash the teeth in the banishment of the
    reprobate,
being miserable, thrice miserable,
with the devils in darkness,
thrust down in the abyss, which even Satan him-
    self dreadeth and abhorreth.

On the one hand
is the vision of God ;
on the other
the hiding of His face.
It is hard to be separated from the saints ;
harder to be severed from God.
It is shameful to be bound and cast out ;
woful to be cast into the fire ;
grievous to call and not to be heard ;
bitter to ask unpitied
for a drop of water, and not obtain it.

Deliver me from all evil and misfortune,
from men of corrupt minds,
from Asshur, from Jeroboam, from Rehoboam,
from the valley of Achor,
from the evil spirit of the men of Shechem,
from every stumblingblock, grief, infamy,
from a deceitful tongue,
from perverse lips,
from snares,
from all enemies, visible, invisible,
corporeal, spiritual,

from vices and sins,
from lusts and temptations,
from the molestation of devils,
from the spirit of fornication,
from the desire of vain glory,
from all defilement of flesh and spirit,
from anger and ill-will,
from polluted thoughts, from blindness of heart.

O Thou, who didst once say to Thy destroying angel,
    It is enough; stay now thine hand:
hear me in my prayers and vows,
    my straits and perils,
    my infirmities and necessities,
    my temptations and tribulations;
repel the concupiscence of gluttony,
    give the virtue of abstinence;
drive away the spirit of fornication,
    give the love of chastity;
extinguish love of the world,
    give poverty of spirit;
restrain headstrong passion,
    quicken in me the spirit of gentleness;
remove the sorrow of this world,
    increase spiritual joy;
repel boastfulness of mind,
    bestow compunction of heart.

Give strength of faith, security of hope,
    the defence of salvation.
Give contempt of the world.

Give me a place among those that shall enter into joy,
    into the joy that is full,
    into the joy that no man taketh away;

that I may have a portion on the right hand,
    in tranquillity,
    in a place of verdure, of dew,
    in paradise,
    in a land of refreshment,
    in Abraham's bosom,
    in the tabernacles of the saints ;
that, being on the right hand of God,
    I may be glad in His rest,
    rejoice in His honour,
    keep holy day in His eternity,
    be glorified by Him that is Thrice-Holy,
    be blessed among His angels,
    and be joyful in His light,
    amidst the psalms above, and songs of heaven.

Give me the girdle, the helmet, the breastplate,
    the shield, the sandals, the sword,
        above all things prayer.

Grant unto me the power and opportunity
        of well doing,
that before the day of my death I may have wrought
  at least somewhat whose good fruit may remain ;
    that I may appear with righteousness,
        and be satisfied with glory.
O Thou that didst add fifteen years
        to the life of Hezekiah,
    grant to me such a space of life,
      at least a sufficient space,
  wherein I may be able to bewail my sins ;
  and, with Thy other blessings, send,
      best gift of all, a good end :
    a good and holy end of life,
  a glorious and joyful resurrection.

Bless our provision from the fruits of the earth and
     its fulness ;
  make peace in our borders ;
  fill us with the finest of the wheat ;
  satisfy our poor with bread ;
  strengthen the bars of our gates ;
  bless our children within us ;
  clothe our enemies with shame ;
  grant us seasonable weather ;
  bestow on us the fruits of the earth ;
  repel carnal desires ;
  restore health to the weak ;
  to the fallen grant restoration ;
  to voyagers and travellers
  a prosperous journey and a port of safety ;
  to the afflicted joy ;
  to the oppressed ease ;
  to the captives liberty ;
  to all health of mind,
  soundness of body.

Another Act of Deprecation.

PUT not Thy servant away in anger,
  nor turn away Thy face, nor hide it.
  nor cover Thyself with a cloud,
  nor shut Thine ear,
  nor forsake me,
  nor leave me for ever,
  nor despise me,
  nor be silent,
  nor slumber,
  nor stand afar off,
  nor cast me off,

nor utterly take Thy lovingkindness from me,
nor suffer Thy faithfulness to fail,
nor rebuke me in Thine anger,
nor chasten me in Thy hot displeasure,
nor cast me away from Thy presence,
nor count me a reprobate from among Thy children,
nor take Thy Holy Spirit from me,
nor forget me for ever,
nor be wroth very sore,
nor shut me up nor consume me in the hand
    of mine iniquity,
nor tarry Thou,
nor gather my soul with sinners.

If by Thy permission we suffer for a while the
    power of the enemy,
    yet let us not in any wise be swallowed up by his
        devouring jaws.
Let the lion be conquered by the lamb,
    the mighty spirit by feeble flesh.

An Act of Pleading.

I. As respects God.

1. from the nature of god.

Because the Lord is merciful and gracious,
    slow to anger, and plenteous in mercy ;
He will not always chide,
    neither will He keep His anger for ever ;
He hath not dealt with us after our sins,
    nor rewarded us according to our iniquities ;
    for as the heaven is high above the earth,
so great is His mercy toward them that fear Him ;
    as far as the east is from the west,

so far hath He removed our transgressions from us;
    like as a father pitieth his children,
      so the Lord pitieth them that fear Him.
Because He is good and ready to forgive,
    and plenteous in mercy unto all them that call
                 upon Him.
The Lord is good to all,
    and His tender mercies are over all His works;
      He delighteth in mercy;
      He is the Father of mercies;
      He is Mercy;
      His nature is to show mercy;
and punishment is His strange and unaccustomed act.

2. FROM THE NAME OF GOD.

Let the power of my Lord be great, according as
Thou hast spoken, saying, The Lord is longsuffering, and of great mercy, forgiving iniquity
and transgression.

3. FROM THE NAME OF FATHER.

I ascend unto my Father, and your Father.
The Father of the prodigal son.
And what wilt Thou do unto Thy great name?

4. FROM THE NAME OF CHRIST.

The typical Lamb.   Behold the Lamb of God!
The Redeemer.   I know that my Redeemer liveth.
The Saviour.   We know that this is indeed the
Saviour of the world.
The Mediator.   There is one Mediator between
God and man.
The Advocate.   We have an Advocate with the
Father.
The Intercessor.   He ever liveth to make inter-
cession.
The High Priest.   We have a great High Priest.

5. FROM THE NAME OF THE HOLY GHOST.

The typical Dove. I saw the Spirit descending from heaven like a dove.

The Anointing. The same anointing teacheth you of all things.

The Comforter. If I go not away, the Comforter will not come unto you.

6. FROM THE PROMISES OF GOD.

Remember the word unto Thy servant,
> upon which Thou hast caused me to hope;
>> which God, that cannot lie, promised,
>>> and confirmed by an oath;
which our unbelief shall not make of none effect;
if we believe not, yet He abideth faithful;
>> He cannot deny Himself.

7. FROM THE PRACTICE OF GOD.

Our fathers trusted in Thee; they trusted in Thee,
> and Thou didst deliver them.
Remember, O Lord, Thy tender mercies,
and Thy lovingkindnesses, for they have been ever of old.
Lord, where are Thy former lovingkindnesses?
Look at the generations of old, and see;
did any ever trust in the Lord, and was confounded?
> did any abide in His fear, and was forsaken?

II. AS RESPECTS OURSELVES, RELATIVELY TO GOD.

1. AS THE WORK AND CREATION OF HIS HANDS.

Forsake not the work of Thine own hands.
> We are the clay, and Thou our potter;
> and we are all the work of Thy hand.
Thou hatest nothing that Thou hast made.

2. AS THE IMAGE OF HIS COUNTENANCE.

Destroy us not.

Let us make man in Our image, after Our likeness.
Who is renewed in knowledge after the image
of Him that created him.

3. AS THE REWARD OF HIS BLOOD.

Despise us not.
Ye are bought with a price,
with the precious blood of a Lamb
without blemish and without spot.

4. AS CALLED BY HIS NAME.

Despise not the express image of Thyself.
We are called by Thy name.
Thy people are called by Thy name.
A chosen vessel, to bear Thy name.

5. AS MEMBERS OF THE BODY OF CHRIST.

Cut us not off.
Ye are the body of Christ, and members in particular.
Know ye not that your bodies are the members
of Christ ?
Know ye not that your body is the temple
of the Holy Ghost Which is in you ?

6. AS HAVING A TITLE IN CHRIST.

I am Thine ; save me.
O Lord, truly I am Thy servant ;
I am Thy servant, and the son of Thine handmaid ;
an unprofitable servant, yet a servant ;
a lost son, yet a son.
We are all Thy people,
Carest Thou not that we perish ? Yea, Thou carest.

III. As RESPECTS OURSELVES, RELATIVELY TO OUR NATURE.

1. FROM OUR WEAKNESS.

Have mercy upon me, O Lord, for I am weak.
> Remember how short my time is.

He remembered that they were but flesh ;
> a wind that passeth away, and cometh not again.

For he knoweth our frame,
> He remembereth that we are dust.

As for man, his days are as grass ;
> as a flower of the field, so he flourisheth.

For the wind passeth over it, and it is gone ;
> and the place thereof shall know it no more.

2. FROM THE MISERY OF OUR CONDITION.

We are brought very low.

And He looked upon them when they were in trouble,
> and heard their prayer.

IV. As RESPECTS OURSELVES, RELATIVELY TO OUR DUE OBEDIENCE.

1. BECAUSE WE REPENT.

A broken and a contrite heart, O God, Thou wilt not despise.

For I will declare mine iniquity ;
> I will be sorry for my sin.

2. BECAUSE WE PRAY.

For I cry unto Thee daily.

How long wilt Thou be angry against the prayer of Thy people?

I forgave thee all that debt, because thou desiredst Me.

3. BECAUSE WE FORGIVE.

Forgive, and ye shall be forgiven.
When ye stand praying, forgive,
                if ye have aught against any :
    that your Father also which is in heaven may
                forgive you your trespasses.
But if ye do not forgive,
        neither will your Father which is in heaven
                forgive your trespasses.

4. BECAUSE WE PURPOSE FOR THE FUTURE.

My soul breaketh for the longing that it hath unto
                Thy judgments at all times.
My hands also will I lift up unto Thy commandments,
                which I have loved.
I have sworn, and I will perform it,
        that I will keep Thy righteous judgments.
Thy servants, who desire to fear Thy name.
That servant, which prepared not himself,
            neither did according to his Lord's will,
                shall be beaten with many stripes.

V. As RESPECTS THE EVIL WHICH WOULD ARISE FROM OUR DESTRUCTION.

1. IT WILL BRING NO ADVANTAGE.

What profit is there in my blood,
                when I go down to the pit ?
                Shall the dust praise Thee ?
                shall it declare Thy truth ?
For in death there is no remembrance of Thee :
    in the grave who shall give Thee thanks ?
            Wilt Thou shew wonders to the dead ?
            shall the dead arise and praise Thee ?
Shall Thy lovingkindness be declared in the grave ?
        or Thy faithfulness in destruction ?

Shall Thy wonders be known in the dark?
and Thy righteousness in the land
of forgetfulness?
For the grave cannot praise Thee, death cannot
celebrate Thee:
they that go down into the pit cannot hope for
Thy truth.
The living, the living, he shall praise Thee.

2. OUR CREATION WILL HAVE BEEN IN VAIN.

Hast Thou made all men for nought?
Enter not into judgment with Thy servant;
for in Thy sight shall no man living be justified.
If Thou, Lord, shouldest mark iniquities,
O Lord, who shall stand?
If He will contend with him,
he cannot answer Him one of a thousand.

3. THE ENEMIES OF GOD WILL TRIUMPH.

Give not Thine heritage to reproach,
that the heathen should rule over them:
wherefore should they say among the people,
Where is their God?
Remember this, that the enemy hath reproached,
O Lord,
and that the foolish people have blasphemed
Thy name.
The tumult of those that rise up against Thee
increaseth continually.
Wherefore should the Egyptians speak, and say,
For mischief did He bring them out,
to slay them in the mountains, and to consume them
from the face of the earth?

The nations which have heard the fame of Thee
will speak, saying,
Because the Lord was not able to bring this people
into the land which He sware unto them ;
therefore He hath slain them in the wilderness.

VI. As respects the good which will arise from our salvation.

1. for the glory of god's name.

Deliver us, O Lord, for the glory of Thy name :
so we Thy people and sheep of Thy pasture
will give Thee thanks for ever :
we will shew forth Thy praise
to all generations.

2. for the conversion of others.

Then will I teach transgressors Thy ways ;
and sinners shall be converted unto Thee.

3. for an example.

For this cause I obtained mercy,
that in me first Jesus Christ might shew forth
all longsuffering,
for a pattern to them which should hereafter believe
on Him
to life everlasting.

4. for the sake of god himself.

I, even I, am He that blotteth out thy transgressions
for Mine own sake.
O Lord, hearken and do ;
defer not, for Thine own sake.
For His sake Whom God hath set forth to be
a propitiation.
Look upon the face of Thine Anointed.
Turn not away the face of Thine Anointed.

5. FOR THE OFFICE OF THE SAVIOUR.

The Spirit of the Lord is upon Me, because He hath
   anointed Me to preach the gospel to the poor;
He hath sent Me
to heal the brokenhearted.
I came to call sinners.
God sent His Son, that the world through Him
might be saved.

Hosanna in the Highest.

A PRAYER FOR THINGS SPIRITUAL.

REMEMBER me, O Lord,
with the favour that Thou bearest unto Thy people;
O visit me with Thy salvation:
that I may see the good of Thy chosen,
that I may rejoice in the gladness of Thy nation,
that I may glory with Thine inheritance.
There is a glory which shall be revealed.

For when the Judge cometh
some shall see Thy face with joy,
shall be placed on the right hand,
shall hear that sweetest word, ' Come, ye blessed.'
They shall be caught up in clouds to meet the Lord;
they shall enter into the joy of their Lord,
they shall enjoy the vision of Him,
they shall be ever with Him.
These alone, only these are blessed
among the sons of men.

O to me the lowest grant the lowest place,
there under their feet,

under the feet of Thy chosen,
the lowest among them.
And that this may be,
let me find grace in Thy sight
to have grace
whereby I may serve Thee acceptably
with reverence and godly fear.
Let me find the grace also
not to receive that grace in vain,
not to come short of it;
yea, not to neglect it,
so as to fall from it;
but to stir it up, so as to grow in it,
yea, to continue in it
till the end of my life.

And O perfect for me
what is lacking of Thy gifts,
increase my little faith,
strengthen my trembling hope,
kindle the smoking flax of my love.
Shed abroad Thy love in my heart
so that I may love Thee,
my friend in Thee, my enemy for Thee.
O Thou Who givest grace to the humble,
give me also grace to be humble.
O Thou Who never failest them that fear Thee,
unite my heart to fear Thy name;
let my heart rejoice in Thy fear.
Let me fear one thing only,
the fearing aught more than Thee.
As I would that men should do to me,
let me do also to them likewise;
let me not think more highly than I ought to think,
but think soberly.

Shine upon them that sit in darkness
and in the shadow of death;
guide our feet into the way of peace,
that we may be of the same mind
one toward another;
and, if in anything we be otherwise minded,
may walk by the same rule,
whereto we have attained;
maintain order,
decency, and steadfastness;
rightly divide, walk uprightly,
edify one another;
with one accord, with one mouth
glorify God.

Hosanna on the Earth.

A PRAYER FOR THINGS TEMPORAL.

REMEMBER, O Lord,
to crown the year with Thy goodness;
for the eyes of all wait upon Thee,
and Thou givest them their meat in due season.
Thou openest Thine hand,
and satisfiest the desire of every living thing.

On us also, O Lord, vouchsafe
the precious things of heaven and the dew above
and the deep that coucheth beneath,
the fruits of the sun, the growth of the moons,
the chief things of the ancient mountains,
the precious things of the everlasting hills,
the precious things of the earth and of its fruit,
good seasons, wholesome weather,

full crops, plenteous fruits,
health of body, peaceful times,
mild government, equal laws,
wise counsels, just judgments,
loyal obedience, vigorous justice,
fertility, fruitfulness,
ease in bearing, happiness in offspring,
careful nurture, sound training;

that our sons may be as plants grown up in their youth,
our daughters as corner stones, polished after the
similitude of a palace:
that our garners may be full,
affording all manner of store:
that our sheep may bring forth thousands
and ten thousands in our streets:
that our oxen may be strong to labour:
that there be no breaking in, nor going out:
that there be no complaining in our streets.
Happy is that people that is in such a case:
yea, happy is that people whose God is the Lord.

An Act of Thanksgiving.

PRAISE waiteth for Thee, O God, in Sion,
and unto Thee shall the vow be performed.
Thou art worthy, O Lord our God, the Holy One,
to receive glory, and honour, and power.
O Thou that hearest prayer,
unto Thee shall all flesh come, shall my flesh come.
Iniquities prevail against me:
as for my transgressions, Thou shalt purge them away,
that I may come and give thanks with all Thy works,
and bless Thee with Thy holy ones.

O Lord, open Thou my lips,
and my mouth shall shew forth Thy praise.

My soul doth praise the Lord
for the goodness He hath done
to the whole creation,
and to the whole race of men;
for Thy mercies towards myself:
soul, body, and estate,
gifts of grace, nature, and worldly good;
for all benefits received,
for all successes, now or heretofore,
for any good thing done;
for health, good report, sufficiency,
safety, freedom, quiet.
Thou hast not cut off as a weaver my life,
nor from day even to night made an end of me.

He hath vouchsafed me life and breath
until this hour,
from childhood, youth, and hitherto,
even unto old age.

Thou holdest my soul in life,
and sufferest not my feet to be moved;
rescuing me from perils, sicknesses,
poverty, bondage, public shame, evil chances;
keeping me from perishing in my sins,
waiting for my full conversion,
leaving in me return into my heart,
remembrance of my latter end,
some shame, horror, grief, for my past sins:
may it be fuller and larger, larger and fuller,
more and still more, O my Lord:
giving me good hopes

of their remission
through repentance and its works,
in the power of the thrice-holy keys,
and the mysteries in Thy Church.

Wherefore day by day for these Thy benefits to me
which I remember,
wherefore also for others very many
which I have let slip,
from their number, from my forgetfulness,
for those which I wished, knew, and asked,
and for those I asked not, knew not, wished not,
I confess and give thanks to Thee,
I bless and praise Thee, as it is meet, and every day;
and I pray with my whole soul,
and with my whole mind I pray.

Glory be to Thee, Lord, glory be to Thee,
glory to Thee, and glory to Thine all-holy name,
for all Thy divine perfections in them:
for Thine unspeakable and unimaginable goodness,
and Thy pity toward sinners
and unworthy,
and toward me, of all sinners
far the most unworthy.

Yea, O Lord, for this, and for the rest,
glory to Thee,
and praise, and blessing, and thanksgiving,
with the voices and concert of voices
of angels and of men,
of all Thy saints in heaven,
and of all Thy creatures in heaven or earth,
and of me, beneath their feet,
unworthy and wretched sinner,

Thy abject creature,
now, in this day and hour,
and every day till my last breath,
and till the end of the world,
and world without end.

Another Act of Thanksgiving.

I.

1. FOR THE EXCELLENCE OF GOD'S MAJESTY.

O FATHER, glorify Thou Me with Thine own self
with the glory which I had with Thee before
the world was.
Melchisedek was priest of the Most High God.

2. HIS EXALTEDNESS.

He that is higher than the highest regardeth.

3. HIS ETERNITY.

The name of the Lord, the Everlasting God.

4. HIS OMNIPRESENCE.

Do not I fill heaven and earth, saith the Lord?

5. HIS OMNISCIENCE.

Whither shall I go from Thy Spirit?
or whither shall I flee from Thy presence?
If I ascend up into heaven, Thou art there;
if I make my bed in hell, behold, Thou art there.
Thou knowest all things.
For Thou, even Thou only, knowest the hearts of all
the children of men.

6. HIS OMNIPOTENCE.

With God nothing shall be impossible.
I am the Almighty God.

7. THE HEIGHT OF HIS WISDOM.

O the depth of the riches both of the wisdom and
knowledge of God!
how unsearchable are His judgments,
and His ways past finding out!

8. HIS UNSHAKEN TRUTH.

The truth of the Lord endureth for ever.
Heaven and earth shall pass away,
but My words shall not pass away.

9. HIS PERFECT RIGHTEOUSNESS.

His righteousness endureth for ever.

10. THE DEPTH OF HIS MERCY.

Deep calleth unto deep.

11. HE IS MERCIFUL IN PASSING BY AND OVER-LOOKING SIN.

I beseech you by the meekness and gentleness of
Christ.
He said, I will not destroy it for ten's sake.
He passeth by transgression.
The times of ignorance God overlooked.

12. HE IS LONGSUFFERING.

Or despisest thou the riches of His forbearance and
longsuffering?

13. HE IS PITIFUL.

But He, being full of compassion, forgave their
iniquity,
and destroyed them not.

14. HE PUNISHETH UNWILLINGLY.

O Ephraim, what shall I do unto thee ?
    O Judah, what shall I do unto thee ?
Many times didst Thou deliver them
        according to Thy mercies.
Many years didst Thou forbear them ;
    Thou didst not utterly consume them,
        nor forsake them.
He hath not dealt with us after our sins,
  neither rewarded us according to our iniquities.
She hath received of the Lord's hand double for all
        her sins.
Like as a father pitieth his children,
    so the Lord pitieth them that fear Him.

15. HE IS COMPASSIONATE.

He repenteth Him of the evil.

16. HIS ANGER IS SOON QUENCHED.

He will not always chide :
    neither will He keep His anger for ever.

17. HE IS READY TO PARDON.

I forgave thee all that debt, because thou
      desiredst Me.

18. HE IS READY TO BE RECONCILED.

Reconciling the world unto Himself,
    not imputing their trespasses unto them.

19. HE IS READY TO BE PROPITIATED.

Bring forth the best robe, and put it on him ;
and put a ring on his hand, and shoes on his feet: etc.
He is kind unto the unthankful and to the evil.

20. HE IS BOUNTIFUL.

Giving the reward of a day for the toil of an hour.
To-day shalt thou be with Me in paradise.
Giving sight to the blind,   loosing the prisoners,
    clothing the naked,   raising the fallen,
    upholding the falling,   healing the sick,
    gathering the dispersed,   feeding the living,
    raising up the bowed down, quickening the dead,
    casting down the proud,   setting up the humble,
    redeeming the captives,   helping in time of need.
Who is like unto Thee, O Lord, among the gods :
glorious in holiness, fearful in praises, doing wonders?

II.

Let us praise God for
    angels, ministering spirits ;
    archangels, bringing great tidings ;
    virtues, doing wonders ;
    powers, defending from devils, at His command ;
    principalities, perfect in government ;
    dominations, bestowing gifts in plenteousness ;
    thrones, that judge ;
    cherubim, shining with knowledge ;
    seraphim, flaming with love ;
    the morning stars,
        rulers of the world,
        lovers of men,
        chief ministers of the divine will.
We praise God for the perseverance of angels ;
    we pray that we, going from strength to strength,
    may be associated with their choirs.

III.

We praise God for
    the patriarchs and their faith,

the prophets and their hope,
the apostles and their labours,
the evangelists and their truth,
the martyrs and their blood,
the confessors and their zeal,
the doctors and their study,
the ascetics and their tears ;
the virgins, flowers of purity,
     celestial gems,
     brides of the immaculate Lamb ;
the innocents and their beauty,
          flowers of the Church,
          mirrors of virtue,
          tabernacles of the Holy Ghost ;
for those whose faith was strong, and whose life
     approved,
          in whose heart was charity,
          in whose mouth verity,
          in whose life piety.

IV.

We praise God
    for light,
        the waters and the firmament,
        the earth and the plants,
        the lights in the firmament of the heaven,
        the fishes and the fowls,
        the wild and tame beasts,
        the rest of the sabbath ;
    for the making of man,
        after counsel held,
        with His own hands ;
    for the breath of life,
        the image of God,
        the dominion over the creatures

the care of the angels,
    his being placed in paradise ;
for that he was not forsaken, when he had sinned ;
for the promise of the seed ;
for that which may be known of God,
    the work of the law written in the heart,
    the oracles of the prophets,
    the melody of the psalms,
    the wisdom of the proverbs,
    the experience of the histories ;

for our birth,
        bringing up,
        preservation,
        direction,
        instruction,
        civilised state,
        religion.

v.

We praise God
    for redemption,
        the great mystery of godliness,
        His making Himself of no reputation,
        His humiliation,
        His taking on Him the seed of Abraham,
        His union to it,
        His oblation of life,
        His sacrifice of death ;
    for all the good that He did,
        all the evil He suffered,
        in His passage from the cradle to the cross ;
    for the whole economy of grace,
        His holy incarnation,
        the poverty of His nativity,
        His lying in the manger,

    His circumcision, subjecting Him to the law,
    His precious name, JESUS,
    His manifestation to sinners of the Gentiles,
    His presentation in the temple,
    His flight into Egypt,
    His consecration of life,
        His desire to hear,
        His eagerness to inquire,
        His humble obedience to His parents;
for His holy baptism,
    the appearance therein of the Trinity,
    His fasting,
    His temptation,
    His poverty, in that He had not where to lay
        His head,
    the hunger and thirst that He endured,
    the cold and heat,
    the weariness, while He went about doing
        good,
    His watchings in prayer,
    His continuance all night in prayer;
for His meek conversation,
    Who endured such contradiction of sinners,
  when He was hurried to the precipice
    for a good word,
  when about to be stoned
    for a good work.

We bless Thee, O Saviour,
    Who didst endure to be insulted of men,
    to be called a Samaritan, a glutton,
    a demoniac, a deceiver,
    and wast content that Barabbas should be
        preferred to Thee,
for Thy sermons, homilies,

> conversations, discourses,
> intercessions, prayers,
> examples,
> signs,
> mysteries,
> the power of the keys;

for the blessings wrought in all the grace and
lovingkindness of Thy miracles;

for the parables of
> the two debtors,
> the good Samaritan,
> the publican and the Pharisee,
> the servant that owed ten thousand talents,
> the lost sheep,
> the prodigal son,
> the called at the eleventh hour;

We bless Thee

for Thy sayings:

>> God sent not His Son into the world to
>> condemn the world; but that the world
>> through Him might be saved.
>>
>> I came not to judge the world, but to save
>> the world.
>>
>> I came not to call the righteous, but sinners
>> to repentance.
>>
>> The Son of Man is not come to destroy men's
>> lives, but to save them.
>>
>> The Son of Man is come to seek and to save
>> that which was lost;
>>
>> and to give His life a ransom for many.
>>
>> Come unto Me, all ye that labour and are
>> heavy laden,
>>
>> and I will give you rest.
>>
>> Him that cometh unto Me I will in no wise
>> cast out.

Father, forgive them; for they know not
what they do.

To-day shalt thou be with Me in paradise.

I will give unto this last even as unto thee.

We bless Thee

for the instances of Thy mercy:

The Syrophenician woman;

the woman of Samaria;

the woman with an issue of blood;

the woman taken in adultery;

Mary Magdalene;

Zacchæus;

the thief;

Peter;

Thomas;

Paul;

Nicodemus.

THIS MAN RECEIVETH SINNERS.

We bless Thee

for Thy longsuffering when

they contradicted Thee;

drew Thee to the brow of the hill;

twice would have stoned Thee;

for a good work blasphemed Thee;

preferred Barabbas unto Thee;

gave Thee up unto the Gentiles to crucify
Thee.

VI.

We praise God

for the death of Christ:

His obedience unto the death of the cross,

His straitening till it was accomplished;

for all that He suffered

in Gethsemane, in Gabbatha, in Golgotha;

for the pain, the shame, the curse
    of the cross.

We praise Him
    that He deigned to be betrayed,
        and that by His own disciple ;
        that He deigned to be sold,
        and that for thirty pieces of silver ;
        to be troubled in His mind,
        to be weary,
        to fear,
        to be exceeding sorrowful, even unto death,
        to be in an agony,
        with strong crying and tears,
        to sweat great drops of blood,
        even to the bedewing of the ground :
                Gethsemane :
        that His disciples should slumber,
        one of them betray Him with a kiss,
        the rest should be offended because of Him,
        and flee ;
        to be left alone,
        and denied by Peter,
        and that with an oath,
        and a curse ;
        to be subjected to the powers of darkness,
        to be laid hands on,
        taken as a thief,
        bound,
        carried away,
        hurried to Annas,
        Caiaphas,
        Pilate,
        Herod,
        Pilate, the second time,

the Prætorium,
Gabbatha,
the cross.

Golgotha :

Thou Who wast silent before the judge,
 restrain my tongue ;
Thou Who didst deign to be bound,
 restrain my hands.

We praise Thee in that
 Thou wast struck with the palm of the hand
  before Annas,
 accused before Caiaphas,
 attacked by false witnesses,
 condemned for blasphemy,
 derided oft,
 mocked by the servants,
 buffeted,
 struck with the palm of the hand,
 wast blindfolded,
 stricken, spit upon,
 reviled, blasphemed ;
We praise Thee in that
 Thy head was crowned with thorns,
  and struck with the reed,
 Thine eyes were dim with tears,
 Thine ears filled with reviling,
 Thy mouth given to drink of gall and vinegar,
 Thy face marred with spitting,
 Thy back ploughed with the scourge,
 Thy neck bent down with the cross,
 Thy hands extended,
 Thy knees bent as in prayer,
 Thy feet pierced with nails,
 Thy heart oppressed with grief,

Thy side pierced with the lance,
Thy blood flowing on all sides plenteously
around Thee,
Thy soul in bitterness,
when Thou criedst in agony, Eli, Eli !

We praise Him that
He deigned to be accused before Pilate of sedition,
to be denied by His own,
rejected for Barabbas ;
He deigned to be sent bound to Herod,
to be clothed with a white robe,
to be mocked ;
He deigned to be sent back to Pilate,
to be clamoured against for death,
to be condemned to a shameful death,
to be given up to the will of the soldiers,
to be arrayed in purple,
to be crowned with thorns,
to be mocked with a reed for a sceptre,
to be bowed the knee to,
to be called King in derision,
to be spit upon,
to be smitten on the head with the reed,
to be stripped of the purple ;
He deigned to be bound to a column in the
judgment hall,
to be beaten with rods,
to be scourged,
to be baptized with a baptism of blood,
to suffer bruises and wounds,
to be demanded with clamour for crucifixion,
to be exhibited as a spectacle of woe,
BEHOLD THE MAN !
to be cried out against the more vehemently,
to be condemned to the cross ;

He deigned to be laden with the cross,
  led to the place of punishment,
  to sink under the cross,
  to have myrrh given Him to drink,
  to endure the shame of being stripped,
  the agony of being extended on the cross,
  to be pierced with nails,
  to have hands and feet riven,
  to be crucified between two thieves,
  to be reckoned among the transgressors,
  to be reviled by the passers by,
 to be blasphemed by the very thieves, on Golgotha;
He deigned to be forsaken of God,
  to be mocked in His cry to God,
  to thirst, to have vinegar given Him to drink,
  to bow His head, and give up the Ghost,
  that His side should be pierced with the spear,
  to be blasphemed after death,
  to be called a deceiver,
  to suffer unknown sufferings.

By Thy woes, which I unworthy here commemorate,
 preserve my soul from the woes of hell.

We praise Him for
 the Seven Last Words:
  1. FATHER, FORGIVE THEM; FOR THEY KNOW
   NOT WHAT THEY DO.
  2. WOMAN, BEHOLD THY SON!
  3. TO DAY SHALT THOU BE WITH ME IN PARADISE.
  4. MY GOD, MY GOD, WHY HAST THOU FORSAKEN
   ME?
  5. I THIRST.
  6. IT IS FINISHED.
  7. FATHER, INTO THY HANDS I COMMEND MY
   SPIRIT.

Thou, who didst deign
   that Thy glorious head should be wounded :
      forgive thereby whatever, by the senses
        of my head, I have sinned ;
   that Thy holy hands should be pierced :
      forgive thereby, whatever I have done amiss
        by unlawful touch, or unlawful act ;
   that Thy precious side should be opened :
      forgive thereby whatever I have offended
        by lawless thoughts, in the ardour of passion ;
   that Thy blessed feet should be riven :
      forgive thereby whatever I have done
        by the means of feet swift to evil ;
   that Thy whole body should be extended :
      forgive thereby whatever iniquity I have com-
        mitted
        by the help of any of my members.

   And I too, O Lord, am wounded in soul ;
       behold the multitude,
    the length, the breadth, the depth,
        of my wounds,
       and by Thine heal mine.

We praise Thee
   for Thy precious death,
      Thy riven side,
      the streams of water and blood,
      the begging of Thy body,
      Thy taking down from the cross,
      Thy burial in the garden of another,
      Thy three days' sepulture.

   By all these things I remind and beseech Thee.
  I pray Thee that Thou wouldest deign to lay all
      these things before Thy Father,

pleading them for my sake :
all the sufferings which Thou barest,
the love above all by which Thou barest.

VII.

We praise Him
  for His exaltation ;
    His triumph over principalities, and leading
              them captive,
    and over the powers of darkness in Himself ;
    His mighty resurrection ;
    His appearance to Mary Magdalene,
      to the women,
      to Peter,
      to the two that went to Emmaus,
      to the ten without Thomas,
      to the eleven,
      at the Sea of Tiberias,
      to James,
      to the five hundred,
      in Bethany ;
    His glorious ascension,
    session at the right hand,
    distribution of gifts,
    continual intercession for us,
    return to judgment.

VIII.

    Come, Holy Ghost, our souls inspire,
    And lighten with celestial fire ;
    Thou the Anointing Spirit art,
    Who dost Thy sevenfold gifts impart.
We praise Thee for
        Thy moving upon the face of the waters,
        Thy emission into all things living ;

Thy inspiration of man,
of Bezaleel,
of the seventy elders,
Thy descent upon the prophets;
Thy visible advent
as a Shadow,
Thy coming upon and overshadowing
at the incarnation of Christ;
as a Dove,
Thy coming in the shape of a dove upon Christ
in baptism;
as fiery Tongues,
after the ascension;
Thy invisible advent
on the apostles gathered together in prayer,
on Cornelius,
on the twelve Ephesians;
Thy often visitations thenceforth
in calling,
calling away from sin,
calling out of the world,
recalling from backsliding,
in our calling on Thee,
in Thy pleading for us;
Thy distribution of graces, ministrations, opera-
tions;
the graces, works, fruits, of the Spirit;
the compunction caused by Thy reproof,
the unction of Thy teaching,
and of Thy bringing to remembrance,
Thy shedding abroad of love,
Thy helping our infirmities, in praying,
Thy witnessing our adoption,
Thy sealing in Thy mysteries,
the earnest of our inheritance;

Thy visiting us, visiting the heart,
>> dwelling in us,
>> purifying us,
>> shining on us, for our illumination,
>> strengthening us,
>> adorning us,
>> carrying us on unto perfection,
> Who guidest us into all truth,
>> and givest us strength.

Another Act of Thanksgiving.

It would rather behove me, O Lord,
> a sinner, and impenitent, and so, wholly unworthy,
>> to lie prostrate before Thee,
> and with tears and groanings to entreat the pardon
>> of my sins,
> than to praise Thee with polluted mouth ;
> yet, trusting in Thine own goodness, I will adore
>> Thee.
>> O receive Thou the praises that it is in my
>> heart to sing.
I praise Thee, I bless Thee, I worship Thee, I
> glorify Thee.
Thou art worthy, O Lord, to receive the praises and
> the thanks,
>> Whom I, a sinner, am unworthy to invoke,
>> or to name, or even to conceive in my heart.

Blessed art Thou, O Lord,
> Who hast created and brought me forth into this life,
> and hast ordered that I should be
>> a living soul and not senseless matter ;
>> a man, not a brute ; civilised, not savage ;
>> free, not a slave ; legitimate, not spurious ;

of honest parents, not of vile extraction, and
as vile myself;
endued with sense, not an idiot;
sound in senses, not blind nor deaf;
sound in limbs, not halt nor maimed;
brought up, not exposed to perish;
liberally educated, not bound to a mechanical
trade;
a Christian, not a pagan;
plucked out of dangers and infamy, not overwhelmed thereby;
in days of peace, not tossed in tempestuous
struggles;
of competent estate, so that I need neither to
flatter nor to borrow;
set free from many sins;
endued with the gifts of grace, in redemption
and calling,
with the gifts of nature and worldly good;

Who according to Thine abundant mercy hast
begotten us again unto a lively hope
by the resurrection of Jesus Christ from the dead,
to an inheritance incorruptible, and undefiled,
and that fadeth not away, reserved in heaven for us;
Who hast blessed me with all spiritual blessings
in heavenly things in Christ;
Who comfortest me in all my tribulation,
for, as the sufferings of Christ have abounded in me,
so my consolation also aboundeth by Christ.

I thank Thee, and praise Thee, O Thou God of my
fathers,
Who hast in some measure given me wisdom and
might,

and hast made known unto me what I desired
of Thee, and hast made known unto me the
king's matter ;
Who hast made me the work of Thine hands,
the reward of Thy blood,
the image of Thy countenance, the servant of
Thy purchase,
a seal of Thy name, a son of Thine adoption,
a temple of Thy Spirit, a member of Thy Church.

An Act of Thanksgiving for the Lord's Day.

O LORD, I am not worthy of the least of all the
mercies,
and all the truth, which Thou hast shewed
unto Thy servant ;
and what can I say more unto Thee ?
for Thou, Lord God, knowest Thy servant.
What is Thy servant, Lord God, and what is
my house,
that Thou hast looked upon such a dead dog as I am,
that Thou hast loved me until now ?
What shall I render unto the Lord for all His
benefits toward me ?
What thanks can we render to God again
for all the joy wherewith we joy before Him ?

Thou who hast deigned, O Lord, to grant me on
this holy day and at this hour
to lift up my soul to Thy praise,
and to give unto Thee the glory due unto Thy name,
receive, O Lord, this spiritual sacrifice from my soul,
and, receiving it to Thee unto Thy spiritual altar,

be pleased in return to shed on me the grace of
Thy Most Holy Spirit.
Visit me in Thy goodness; forgive me every sin,
whether willingly or unwillingly committed.
Deliver me from eternal punishment;
yea, and from all the miseries of this world.
Change my thoughts into piety;
sanctify my spirit, soul and body;
and give me grace to worship and to please Thee
in piety and holiness of life
even unto the very end of my days.

Unto Him that is able to do exceeding abundantly
above all that we ask or think,
according to the power that worketh in us,
unto Him be glory in the Church by Christ Jesus
throughout all ages, world without end.

My soul shall be satisfied as with marrow and fatness;
and my mouth shall praise Thee with joyful lips.

A Meditation on the Aggravation of Sin.

Its measure,
its harm,
its scandal,
its quality,
its iteration, how often?
its continuation, how long?
The person by whom:
his age, condition, state, enlightenment.
Its manner, its motive,
its time, its place,
its folly, ingratitude, hardness, contempt.

The various kinds of sin :
  the cord and the cart rope ;
  in necessary things,
  in things superfluous ;
  omission or defect,
      the not doing what ought to be done,
  commission, or excess,
      the doing what ought not to be done ;
  by heart within, in thought ;
  by mouth without, in word,
  by deed without, in fact ;
  against God, my neighbour, my own body ;
  by knowledge and by ignorance ;
  willingly and unwillingly ;
  of old and of late ;
  in boyhood and youth,
  in mature and old age ;
  things done once, repeated often ;
  hidden and open ;
  things done in anger,
  or from the lust of the flesh and the world ;
  before and after my call ;
  asleep by night, and awake by day ;
  things concerning myself alone,
  and things connected with others ;
  things remembered, and things forgotten.

Whatsoever I have done amiss, from my youth
        till now, till this moment,
      knowingly or ignorantly, within or without,
        asleep or awake,
      by words, deeds, or thoughts,
      through the fiery darts of the enemy,
      through the unclean desires of the flesh,
  have mercy on me, O God, and forgive me.

A Meditation on the Day of Judgment.

FATHER unoriginate, only begotten Son,
life-giving Spirit,
merciful, compassionate, longsuffering,
full of pity, full of tender yearnings,
Who lovest the just and pitiest the sinful,
Who passest by sins and grantest petitions,
God of penitents,
Saviour of sinners,
I have sinned before Thee, O Lord,
and thus and thus have I done.
Alas, alas! woe, woe!
how was I enticed by my own lust,
how I hated instruction.
Nor felt I fear nor awe
of Thy incomprehensible glory,
Thy dread presence,
Thy terrible power,
Thy strict justice,
Thy winning goodness.

I will call if there be any that will answer me ;
to which of the holy angels shall I turn ?
O wretched man that I am,
who shall deliver me from the body of this death ?
How fearful is Thy judgment, O Lord,
when the thrones are set,
and the angels in presence,
and men brought in,
the books opened,
the works inquired into,
the thoughts examined,
and the hidden things of darkness.

What judgment shall be upon me,
    who shall quench my flame,
    who shall lighten my darkness,
       if Thou pity me not?

Lord, as Thou art the Lover of men, give me tears,
    give me floods, give them to-day.

For then will be the incorruptible Judge,
       the awful judgment seat,
       the answer without excuse,
       the inevitable charges,
       the bitter punishment,
       the endless Gehenna,
       the pitiless angels,
       the yawning hell,
       the roaring stream of fire,
         of fire unquenchable,
       the dark prison,
       the rayless darkness,
       the bed of live coals,
       the unwearied worm,
       the indissoluble chains,
       the immeasurable gulf,
       the impassable wall,
       the inconsolable cry :
none to stand by me, none to plead for me,
       none to snatch me out.

But I repent, Lord; O Lord, I repent;
    help Thou mine impenitence,
and more, and still more, pierce, rend, crush my heart.
Behold, O Lord, that I am indignant with myself
    for my senseless, profitless,
       hurtful, perilous passions;

that I abhor myselt
for the inordinate, unseemly,
deformed, deceitful,
shameful, disgraceful
thing that is in me ;
that my confusion is continually before me,
and the shame of my face hath covered me.
Alas ! woe, woe !
O me, how long ?
Behold, Lord, that I judge myself worthy
of everlasting punishment,
yea, and of all miseries of this world.
Behold me, Lord, self-condemned ;
behold, Lord, and enter not into judgment
with Thy servant.

And now, Lord,
I humble myself under Thy mighty hand ;
I bow my knees unto Thee, O Lord,
I fall on my face to the earth.
Let this cup pass from me.
I stretch forth my hands unto Thee ;
I smite upon my breast, upon my thigh.
Out of the depths my soul crieth unto Thee,
as a thirsty land,
and all my bones,
and all that is within me.
Lord, hear my voice.

A Meditation on the Shortness of Life.

HAVE mercy upon me, O Lord, for I am weak.
Remember, Lord, how short my time is ;
remember that I am but flesh,
a wind that passeth away, and cometh not again.

My days are as grass, as a flower of the field;
for the wind passeth over me, and I am gone,
and my place shall know me no more.
For I am dust and ashes,
earth and grass,
flesh and breath,
corruption and a worm;
as a stranger upon the earth,
dwelling in a house of clay;
few and evil my days,
to-day, and not to-morrow,
in the morning, yet not until night;
in a body of sin,
in a world of corruption;
of few days, and full of trouble,
coming forth and cut down like a flower,
fleeing also as a shadow, and continuing not.

Remember this, O Lord, and suffer, pardon:
for what profit is there in my blood,
when I go down to the pit?
by the multitude of Thy tender mercies,
the riches and exceeding abundance
of Thy compassions.

By all that is dear to Thee, all that we should plead,
and, before and beyond all things, by Thyself,
by Thyself, O Lord, and by Thy Christ,
Lord, have mercy upon me, the chief of sinners.
O my Lord, let Thy mercy rejoice
against Thy judgment in my sin.
O Lord, hear; O Lord, forgive;
O Lord, hearken; O Lord, hearken and do;
do and defer not for Thine own sake;
defer not, O Lord my God.

A Prayer of Thomas Bradwardine, Archbishop of Canterbury.

THYSELF, my God, I love, Thyself for Thyself, above all things. For Thyself I long. Thyself I desire as a final end. Thyself, for Thyself, not for aught else, I always and in all things seek with my heart and whole strength, with groaning and weeping, with continual labour and grief. What therefore wilt Thou give me as my final end? If Thou dost not bestow on me Thyself, Thou bestowest on me nothing. If Thou dost not give me Thyself, Thou givest me nothing. If I find not Thyself, I find nothing. Thou dost not then reward me, but torturest me. For even before that I sought Thee, I hoped to find and possess Thee at last. And with this honeyed hope I was sweetly consoled in all my labours. But now, if Thou deniest me Thyself, and that for ever, and not for a season, whatever else Thou shalt give me, shall I not always languish with love, mourn with languishing, grieve with mourning, weep with grieving, because I shall ever remain void and empty? Shall I not mourn inconsolably, complain unceasingly, grieve interminably? That is not Thy wont, God of goodness, of clemency, and love; it is in no wise fitting, in no point seemly. Grant, therefore, O my gracious God, that in the present life I may ever love Thyself, for Thyself, above all things, seek Thee in all things, and in the world to come may find Thee, and keep hold of Thee for ever.

COMMUNION PRAYERS AND
MEDITATIONS

An Act of Self=Examination before the Lord's Supper.

HAVE I penitence, grief, shame, pain, horror, weariness, for my sin?
Do I pray, if not seven times, as David,
yet at least thrice, as Daniel?
If not, as Solomon, at length,
yet shortly, as the publican?
If not, like Christ, the whole night,
at least for one hour?
If not on the ground, and in ashes,
at least not in my bed?
If not in sackcloth,
at least not in purple and fine linen?
If not altogether freed from all,
at least from immoderate, desires?
Do I give, if not, as Zaccheus, fourfold,
at least, as the law commands, with the fifth
part added?
if not as the rich, yet as the widow?
if not the half, yet the thirtieth part?
if not above my power, yet up to my power?

An Act of Prayer before the Lord's Supper.

LORD, I am not worthy, I am not fit,
that Thou shouldest come under the defiled roof
of my soul,

for it is all desolate and ruined;
nor hast Thou in me fitting place
to lay Thy head.

But, as Thou didst condescend
to lie in the cavern and manger of brute cattle,
as Thou didst not refuse
to be entertained in the house of Simon the leper,
as Thou didst not disdain
the harlot, a sinner like me,
when she came to Thee and touched Thee,
as Thou abhorredst not
her polluted and loathsome mouth,
nor the thief upon the cross
confessing Thee:
so even me, the ruined, wretched,
and excessive sinner,
deign to receive to the touch and the partaking
of the immaculate, supernatural, life-giving,
and saving mysteries
of Thy all-holy body
and Thy precious blood.

Listen, O Lord, our God,
from Thy holy habitation,
and from the glorious throne of Thy kingdom,
and come to sanctify us.
O Thou Who sittest on high with the Father,
and art present with us here invisibly,
come Thou to sanctify the gifts which lie before Thee,
and those in whose behalf, and by whom,
and the things for which,
they are brought near Thee.
And grant to us communion,
unto faith without shame,

love unfeigned,
fulfilment of Thy commandments,
readiness to bring forth every spiritual fruit,
deliverance from all that is adverse,
healing of soul and body;
that we too, with all saints
since the world began
who have been well pleasing to Thee,
may become partakers
of Thy undefiled and everlasting goods,
which Thou hast prepared, O Lord, for them that
love Thee;
in whom Thou art glorified for ever and ever.

O Lamb of God,
Which takest away the sin of the world,
take away the sin of me,
the utter sinner.

A Meditation during this Service and after the Supper.

A TOKEN of fellowship.   *Acts* ii. 42.
A memorial of the dispensation.   *Luke* xxii. 19, 20.
A shewing of the Lord's death.   1 *Cor.* xi. 26.
The communion of His body and blood.
    1 *Cor.* x. 16.
A sharing in the Spirit.   1 *Cor.* xii. 13.
Remission of sins.   *Matt.* xxvi. 28.
Purging out of things contrary.   1 *Cor.* v. 7.
Rest of conscience.   *Matt.* xi. 28.
Blotting out of debts.   *Col.* ii. 14.
Cleansing of stains.   *Heb.* ix. 14.
Healing of the soul's sicknesses.   1 *Pet.* ii. 24.

Renewing of the covenant.   *Psalm* l. 5.
Food of spiritual life.   *John* vi. 27.
Increase of strengthening grace.   *Heb.* xiii. 9.
And of soul-winning consolation.   *Phil.* ii. 1.
Compunction of penitence.   2 *Cor.* vii. 9.
Illumination of mind.   *Luke* xxiv. 31.
Exercise of humility.   *John* xiii. 11.
Seal of faith.   2 *Cor.* i. 22.
Fulness of wisdom.   *John* vi. 35.
Bond of love.   *John* xiii. 35.
Arming with endurance.   1 *Peter* iv. 1.
Liveliness of thanksgiving.   *Psalm* cxvi. 12.
Confidence of prayer.   *Psalm* cxvi. 13.
Mutual indwelling.   *John* vi. 56.
Pledge of resurrection.   *John* vi. 54.
Acceptable defence in judgment.   1 *Cor.* xi. 29.
Covenant of the inheritance.   *Luke* xxii. 20.
Figure of perfection.   *John* xvii. 23.

Communion.

WE then remembering, O sovereign Lord,
    in the presence of Thy holy mysteries,
    the saving sufferings of Thy Christ,
    His life-giving cross,
    most precious death,
    three days' burial,
    resurrection from the dead,
    ascension into heaven,
    sitting at the right hand of Thee, the Father,
    His glorious and terrible coming,
        beseech Thee, O Lord,
    that we, receiving in the pure testimony
            of our conscience
        our portion of Thy sacred things,

may be made one with the holy body and blood
of Thy Christ;
and, receiving them not unworthily,
may hold Christ dwelling in our hearts,
and may become a temple
of Thy Holy Spirit.
Yea, O our God.

Nor make any of us guilty
of these Thy dread and heavenly mysteries,
nor infirm in soul or body
from partaking of them unworthily.
But grant us
until our last and closing breath
worthily to receive a hope of Thy holy things,
for sanctification, enlightenment, strengthening;
for relief of the burden of my many sins,
safeguard against all Satanic working,
deliverance from my evil conscience,
mortification of my passions;
for fulfilment of Thy commandments,
growth in Thy divine grace,
and possession of Thy kingdom.

After Communion.

FULFILLED and finished,
so far as in our power,
O Christ our God,
is the mystery of Thy dispensation.

For we have held remembrance of Thy death,
we have seen the figure of Thy resurrection,
we have been filled with Thy endless life,

we have enjoyed Thy uncloying dainties,
of which graciously vouchsafe unto all of us
to be accounted worthy also
in the world to come.

The good Lord
pardon every one
that prepareth his heart to seek God,
the Lord God of his fathers,
though he be not cleansed
according to the purification of the sanctuary.